# A Treasury of Whole Language

# LITERATURE IDEAS

Barbara Reeves

**Troll Associates**

Interior Illustrations by: Doug Roy

ISBN: 0-8167-2585-3

Printed in the United States of America.

10  9  8  7  6  5  4

# CONTENTS

# INTRODUCTION

Reading can open up a world of enjoyment and wonder to children, but how can you encourage your students to become enthusiastic readers? One way to accomplish that goal is to introduce students to valued works of literature that interest and excite them—literature that will help them develop a true love of reading.

**A Treasury of Whole Language Literature Ideas** is a collection of activities that will help your students become involved with literature while developing important whole language skills. The twenty-two books around which the activities are based are well-known, popular selections, many of which have won honors such as Caldecott and Newbery awards. Depending on the book and the abilities of your students, literature selections may be presented to the class as a whole or to individual reading groups.

**A Treasury of Whole Language Literature Ideas** includes some of the following features for each book:

*Summary* A summary is provided for each book to help you choose appropriate literature for your students. Use the summary to become acquainted with the book if you are not already familiar with it. It is also suggested that you read or preview each book before presenting it to students.

*Discussion Sparklers* Discussion Sparklers are questions that you may use to initiate discussions and to tap higher-level thinking skills. Talk about the questions after students have read the book or at key points in the reading.

*For Your Bulletin Board* As students are reading the book, follow the bulletin board suggestion to help bring a visual focus to the literature and to spark interest and creativity.

*Fun Fact* Facts that relate to the literature are interspersed throughout *A Treasury of Whole Language Literature Ideas*. Incorporate the facts into your teaching to increase students' knowledge of story concepts and to present interesting and entertaining information.

*Read It Aloud!/Act It Out!* A Read It Aloud! or Act It Out! feature is included for each book. Use the feature after students have read the book at least once. Read It Aloud! suggests a read-aloud opportunity for students. Act It Out! gives a suggestion for dramatizing the literature.

**Curriculum Connection Activities** Included are activities that connect to curriculum areas such as mathematics, science, social studies, language arts, music, art, physical education, and cooking. Present the activities after students have read the book to support, extend, and enrich the reading experience and to tap whole language skills such as speaking, listening, reading, and writing.

**Other Books to Enjoy** You may wish to provide students with the books listed in this bibliography to extend concepts and to promote independent reading.

**Activity Sheets** The two reproducible activity sheets are designed so that students may complete them independently after reading the book. However, at early reading levels, you may wish to guide students through the work. A major focus of the activity sheets is to provide students with the opportunity to express themselves creatively while developing writing and speaking skills.

**Book Report Forms** Provide students with copies of the two reproducible book report forms so that they may share their opinions of books with one another. Use Book Report Form 1 for students with limited writing abilities and Book Report Form 2 for more advanced students. You may wish to have students display their book reports in class or read them aloud.

# ABEL'S ISLAND
### Written and Illustrated by William Steig

### SUMMARY

Abel is a mouse who has always enjoyed the best things in life. His comfortable lifestyle changes suddenly one day, when he and his wife Amanda go on a picnic. A violent storm arises, and he is swept away while running after Amanda's scarf. Floodwaters carry Abel to an island, where he finds himself alone and stranded. Now Abel must learn to survive on his own, enduring loneliness and the harshness of nature. As a year passes, Abel learns new skills and gains an appreciation for the world around him. Eventually he figures out a way to leave the island and return home. Time on the island changes Abel, however, and he comes away with a new purpose in life and a love for the island that sheltered him.

**Discussion Sparklers**

1 How do you think Abel's life changed after he returned from the island? In what ways might his lifestyle have been different? In what ways might it have remained the same?

2 Imagine that you were swept away to an island where nobody lived. If you could have three things with you on the island, what would those things be? Give reasons for your answers.

3 Have you ever been on a small island? Describe what it was like. How would your life be different if you lived on a small island?

# FOR YOUR BULLETIN BOARD

Review Chapter 4 of *Abel's Island* with students, discussing the different kinds of watercraft that Abel built. Point out the picture of the raft and the catamaran. Then invite students to draw a picture of what they think Abel's sailboat looked like. Encourage students to base their drawings on information from the chapter. Post the drawings on a bulletin board labeled "Abel's Sailboat."

# Fun Fact

Can you name the largest island in the world? It's Greenland in the North Atlantic, with an area of 840,000 square miles (2,175,600 km²). Despite its name, Greenland is a cold, icy place. In fact, most of the island is covered with a permanent ice cap!

*Read It Aloud!* Ask students to go back to the part of the book they enjoyed the most and choose two or three paragraphs to read aloud. Encourage students first to read the paragraphs silently and then practice reading aloud with a partner. When students are ready, have them read aloud to the class.

*Art Connection* Remind students that while Abel was on the island, he made statues of his loved ones. Provide students with self-hardening modeling clay or dough and invite them to make small statues of characters from the book, such as Abel, Amanda, Gower, the owl, or the cat. When the clay or dough hardens, have students paint the statues. Display the statues on a table or shelf in the classroom.

*Science Connection* Point out to students that there are four different kinds of islands—*barrier islands, continental islands, coral islands,* and *volcanic islands.* Divide the class into four groups and challenge each group to find out how one type of island is formed. Help students by providing a set of encyclopedias and books about islands. As an alternative, take a class trip to the library to do research. Invite each group to report its findings to the class.

*Mathematics Connection* Remind students that Abel used his tail to measure the length and width of the island. Then have students cut a piece of string the length of their arm, from fingertip to shoulder. Have them use the string to measure the length or width of the classroom. Invite students to compare results and discuss how their measurements vary. Next, have students measure the room in feet and inches (or in meters and centimeters). Point out the importance of using uniform units of measurement such as feet, inches, meters, and centimeters to obtain accurate measurements that do not vary.

## Other Books to Enjoy

Rydell, Wendy. *All About Islands.* Troll, 1984.

Seidler, Tor. *A Rat's Tale.* Farrar, Straus, 1986.

Simon, Seymour. *Storms.* Morrow, 1989.

Taylor, Kim. *Secret Worlds: Hidden Under Water.* Doubleday, 1990.

White, E. B. *Stuart Little.* Harper, 1945.

*Answers to Activity Sheet 1:*
**1.** cerulean **2.** abominable **3.** raiment **4.** catamaran
**5.** ensconced **6.** incantation **7.** somnolent **8.** maelstrom
**9.** catapult **10.** vocation **11.** rime **12.** fop

| A | m | a | n | d | a's | | s | c | a | r | f |
|---|---|---|---|---|---|---|---|---|---|---|---|
| 1 | 2 | 3 | 4 | 5 | 6 | 7 | 8 | 9 | 10 | 11 | 12 |

Name _____ Date _____

# Abel's Words

▶ Write each word from *Abel's Island* in the boxes next to the correct definition. Use a dictionary to help you if needed.

ABEL'S ISLAND

| abominable | catamaran | catapult | cerulean | ensconced | fop |
| incantation | maelstrom | raiment | rime | somnolent | vocation |

**1.** sky blue ☐☐☐☐☐☐▨☐

**2.** disgusting, detestable ☐☐☐▨☐☐☐☐☐

**3.** clothing ☐▨☐☐☐☐☐

**4.** raft made of wood or logs tied together ☐☐☐☐☐☐☐☐▨

**5.** comfortably settled ☐☐☐☐☐☐☐▨

**6.** words used to produce a magic effect ☐☐☐▨☐☐☐☐☐☐

**7.** sleepy, drowsy ▨☐☐☐☐☐☐☐☐

**8.** whirlpool, powerful force ☐☐☐☐▨☐☐☐☐

**9.** throw or launch ▨☐☐☐☐☐☐☐

**10.** occupation, life's work ☐☐☐▨☐☐☐☐

**11.** frost ▨☐☐☐

**12.** dandy, vain person ▨☐☐

▶What began and ended Abel's adventure? To find out, write the letters from the shaded boxes above in the blanks below. Capitalize the first letter and add punctuation where needed.

___ ___ ___ ___ ___ ___ ___   ___ ___ ___ ___ ___
 1   2   3   4   5   6   7     8   9   10  11  12

# A Letter from Gower

▶ Imagine that Gower wrote a letter to Amanda when he returned home, but forgot to send it to her! What do you think Gower would have said in his letter? Write the letter for Gower.

16 Lily Pad Lane
Riverside, U.S.A.

Dear Amanda,

Sincerely,
Gower Glackens

# ARROW TO THE SUN

Adapted and Illustrated by Gerald McDermott

### SUMMARY

In this Pueblo Indian tale, the Lord of the Sun sends the spark of life to earth, creating a son who is born to a young maiden. As the boy grows, he is mocked by others in the pueblo because he is fatherless. Saddened, the boy leaves to search for his father. In his travels the boy meets wise Arrow Maker, who makes a special arrow to send the boy into the heavens. There, the boy meets his father, the Lord of the Sun, who says the boy must prove himself by passing through four chambers of ceremony. The boy endures the trials of the chambers and emerges transformed, filled with the sun's power. The boy and his father rejoice, and the boy returns to earth, bringing the spirit of the sun to the world.

## Discussion Sparklers

1 Why do you think Corn Planter and Pot Maker would not speak to the boy when he asked them if they could lead him to his father? Why do you think Arrow Maker was able to see that the boy came from the sun?

2 Look at the pictures of the boy in the chambers of ceremony. What do you think happened when he went into each kiva? Which kiva would be most frightening to you? Tell why.

3 Why do you think the people of the pueblo celebrated the boy's return with the Dance of Life?

## FOR YOUR BULLETIN BOARD

Ask students to think about a message that they would like to send to the sun. Suggest messages such as "I like it when you shine" or "Thanks for making the plants grow!" Then invite students to draw and cut out their own special arrow to the sun. Have them write their message on the arrow and decorate the arrow with Pueblo Indian designs such as those in the book. Post a large cutout of the sun on a bulletin board labeled "Messages to the Sun." Have students arrange their arrows on the bulletin board pointing toward the sun.

# Fun Fact

The word *pueblo* means "town" or "village" in Spanish. Spanish explorers used the word to refer to the villages that the Pueblo Indians built, as well as to the people themselves. The ancestors of the Pueblo Indians are called the *Anasazi*, a Navajo word that means "the old ones."

*Act It Out!* Have students work in small groups to act out *Arrow to the Sun*. Remind them to select a narrator. To add interest to the dramatization, students may make character masks from paper bags and wear them during their performance.

## Social Studies Connection Invite
students to create their own pueblo. Provide them with cardboard boxes of various sizes and have them cut out windows and doors to make the boxes look like rooms in a pueblo. Have groups of students tape their boxes together to form a multistory dwelling. Ladders for the pueblo may be made from pipe cleaners, and clothespins may be used as figures of people.

## Science Connection Point out to
students that the sun is actually 93 million miles (150 million km) from the earth. Then talk about how the rotation of the earth creates day and night. To demonstrate the concept, mark where you live on a globe. In a dark room, shine a bright light (the sun) on the globe as you turn it. As an alternative, you may also use a large ball as the earth, turning the ball in your hands to demonstrate night and day. Next, invite a volunteer to move the globe or ball around the light source to demonstrate how the earth revolves around the sun once a year.

## Language Arts Connection Have
students work together to create their own oral folk tale about a girl whose mother is the moon. Ask students to sit in a circle and invite a volunteer to begin the tale. Encourage students to take turns adding to the story. If possible, record the tale as it is told and play it back for students to enjoy.

## Other Books to Enjoy

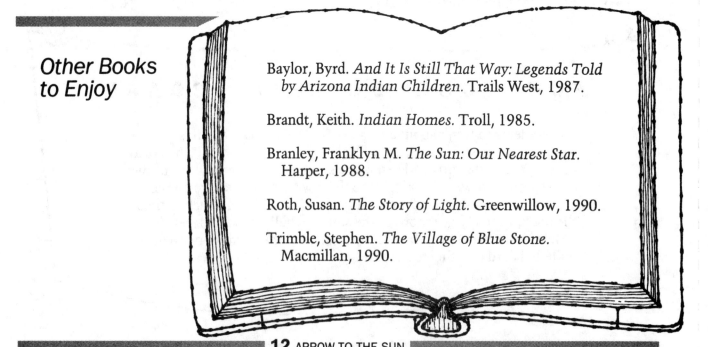

Baylor, Byrd. *And It Is Still That Way: Legends Told by Arizona Indian Children.* Trails West, 1987.

Brandt, Keith. *Indian Homes.* Troll, 1985.

Branley, Franklyn M. *The Sun: Our Nearest Star.* Harper, 1988.

Roth, Susan. *The Story of Light.* Greenwillow, 1990.

Trimble, Stephen. *The Village of Blue Stone.* Macmillan, 1990.

# Picture a Pueblo

▶ Read the definitions below. Use the words to label the picture.

**beam** (bēm)   Long piece of wood that supports part of a building.

**hatchway** (**hach**-wā)   An opening or door in a floor or a roof.

**kiva** (**kē**-və)   Room for ceremonies, often round and underground.

**maize** (māz)   Indian corn.

**mesa** (**mā**-sə)   Elevated land with a flat top and steep sides.

**terrace** (**ter**-əs)   Flat roof that is used like a balcony.

▶ Work with a partner. Take turns telling stories about the pueblo in the picture.

Name _____    Date _____

# Be a Pot Maker

▶ Decorate the pot to show a story of your own. Use designs and figures like those in the book.

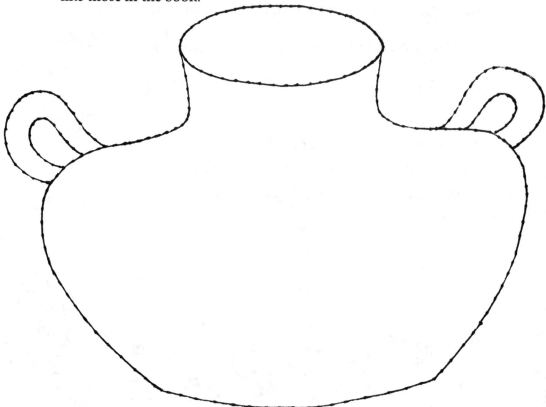

▶ Write the story that you drew on the pot or tell your story to your classmates.

_____

_____

_____

_____

_____

_____

_____

# ASHANTI TO ZULU

### Written by Margaret Musgrove
### Illustrated by Leo and Diane Dillon

## SUMMARY

The culture of twenty-six different African peoples is celebrated in this book of vignettes. An important custom of each group of people is introduced, giving the reader a feeling for the richness and variety of African life. From the Ashanti tradition of weaving beautiful cloth, to the Masai men's custom of wearing tiny braids, to the complicated dances of the Zulu, the author describes customs unique to a particular people as well as those shared by many peoples throughout Africa.

## Discussion Sparklers

**1** Which group of African people is the most interesting to you? Why do you find that group interesting?

**2** Are any of the traditions and customs mentioned in the book similar to those that we follow in our own country? How are they alike? How are they different?

**3** What do the pictures in the book tell you about family life in Africa? What do they tell you about the kinds of animals found there?

**4** How did the author organize the information in this book? Do you think her method of organization was a good one? Tell why or why not.

## FOR YOUR BULLETIN BOARD

Invite students to "dress" themselves as a member of one of the African peoples. Have them paste a photograph of their face in the middle of a piece of paper. (As an alternative, students may draw their face on the paper.) Then have them draw their body dressed in the traditional clothes of one of the peoples. Below the picture have students write the name of the group from which the clothing comes. Post the pictures on a bulletin board labeled "African Clothing."

*Read It Aloud!* Write all the letters of the alphabet on slips of paper and put the papers in a bag or hat. Invite each student to choose a letter and read aloud the corresponding portion of the book.

## Social Studies Connection

Use the map at the back of the book to help students locate the homes of the African people that they read about. Then display a globe or an atlas and have students take turns locating various countries in Africa as you name them. Encourage students to locate the Nile River, the Congo River, and Lake Victoria. Then challenge students to use the map or globe to pose riddles to each other. For example, a student might say, "I am thinking of a country that is south of Egypt and east of Chad. Which country is it?" (Sudan) "I am thinking of a country on the Indian Ocean. Its name starts with *T*." (Tanzania)

## Physical Education Connection

Remind students that the Vai people of Liberia carry almost everything on their heads. Then invite students to try the skill themselves! Have them begin by balancing a book on their head and walking across the room. Then encourage them to add unbreakable objects on top of the book and attempt to walk across the room without touching the objects or dropping them.

## Music Connection

Discuss with students the way the Ewe drummers make their drums "talk." Then provide students with drums to play or have them make their own drums from coffee tins with plastic lids, cylindrical oatmeal containers, or plastic bowls of various sizes. Invite partners to play their drums together, creating drumbeats that represent sounds such as rain and thunder; people talking, walking, and marching; and animals running or roaring. Have partners demonstrate their talking drums to the class. You might also read aloud passages from poetry and have students accompany the words with drumbeats.

## Art Connection

Have students make an African animal collage. Ask each student to choose one animal from the book and draw it on paper. Have students color their pictures and cut them out. Then invite students to paste all the pictures on a large sheet of chart paper or butcher paper to form a collage. Post the collage on a wall under the banner "Animals of Africa."

## Other Books to Enjoy

Georges, D. V. *Africa.* Childrens, 1986.

Griffin, Michael. *A Family in Kenya.* Lerner, 1988.

Lye, Keith. *Take a Trip to Nigeria.* Watts, 1984.

McKenna, Nancy Durrell. *A Zulu Family.* Lerner, 1986.

*Answers to Activity Sheet 1:*
*Across:* 1. Wagenia 4. Pondo 5. Zulu 7. Fanti 8. Rendille 11. Ndaka 12. Jie
*Down:* 2. Ashanti 3. Ikoma 6. Uge 9. Dogon 10. Masai

Name _____    Date _____

# Crossing Africa

▶ Complete the crossword puzzle with the names in the box. Use the clues below the puzzle and the book *Ashanti to Zulu* to help you.

| ASHANTI | DOGON | FANTI | IKOMA |
| JIE | MASAI | NDAKA | PONDO |
| RENDILLE | UGE | WAGENIA | ZULU |

**ACROSS**

1. Fishermen use catwalks over the Congo River
4. Boys love to spar with sticks
5. Have beautiful dances for all occasions
7. Make white bubbly palm wine
8. Live in movable houses
11. Brides are wrapped in yards and yards of cloth
12. Herders in Uganda

**DOWN**

2. Weave cloth called *kente*
3. Gather honey to eat and sell
6. Collect and chew kola nuts
9. Farmers who live in Mali
10. Women shave their heads and wear pounds of jewelry

# Family Traditions

▶ Draw a picture of a tradition that your family enjoys. Below the picture describe the tradition.

Family Name: _____

Tradition: _____

_____

_____

_____

_____

_____

▶ Work with your classmates. Alphabetize your papers by family names. Bind the papers into a booklet titled *Families and Traditions.*

# CAPS FOR SALE

Written and Illustrated by Esphyr Slobodkina

### S U M M A R Y

A cap peddler wanders through the streets of a town, selling caps that he wears on his head. One morning the peddler goes for a walk in the country and falls asleep under a tree. When he wakes, all of the caps are gone, except for his own checked cap, which remains on his head. Looking up into the tree, the peddler sees a bunch of monkeys—each wearing one of the caps! The peddler scolds the monkeys, shakes his finger and hands at them, and stamps his feet. But the monkeys only mimic what he does, and the caps stay on their heads. Finally, in anger, the peddler pulls off his own cap and throws it on the ground. The monkeys do the same! The peddler picks up all his caps and returns to town.

1 Have you ever seen people selling things on the streets of your city or town? What did they sell? Talk about what you saw and heard.

3 Might you ever see monkeys sitting in a tree where you live? Where have you seen real monkeys? How did they act? Were they at all like the monkeys in the story?

2 Do you think it was a good idea for the peddler in the story to carry all his caps on his head? Why or why not? How else might the peddler have carried his caps?

# F O R   Y O U R   B U L L E T I N   B O A R D

Invite students to create fanciful caps of their own—ones that would attract the attention of a bunch of curious monkeys! Have each student draw a cap on construction paper, cut it out, and decorate it with crayons or markers. Then draw the outline of a large tree on the bulletin board. Label the board "Caps for Sale" and have students post their caps on the tree.

# Fun Fact

Did you know there are two types of monkeys—Old World monkeys and New World monkeys? Old World monkeys live in Africa and Asia. New World monkeys live in Central and South America. Only New World monkeys have tails that can hold onto things, so only New World monkeys can hang from their tails!

*Act It Out!* Pass out paper plates and have each student create a monkey mask and a peddler mask. Help students attach string to the masks so that they can be worn. Then invite small groups of students to act out the story while wearing the masks. Students may take turns playing the part of the peddler. You may wish to provide caps for the "peddler" and the "monkeys" to wear.

*Cooking Connection* Have students make Monkey Hash. Supply them with ingredients such as nuts, banana chips, dried fruits, marshmallows, and coconut. (Students may also bring ingredients from home.) Have students work in small groups to mix the ingredients and make this special snack.

*Social Studies Connection* Stage a peddler's fair for parents or other classes. Work with students to create items to display at the fair, such as clay monkeys, paper caps, bags of Monkey Hash, tissue-paper flowers, or monkey puppets made from socks or paper bags. You may wish to have students price the items and sell them at the fair. Then use the money for a special class outing—perhaps to the zoo!

*Mathematics Connection* Play the part of the peddler in the story and have students use play coins to buy caps from you. For example, call out "Caps! Caps for sale! Five cents a cap!" Then ask students to show the coins they would need to buy one cap, two caps, three caps, and so on. Vary the activity by calling out different prices.

## Other Books to Enjoy

Arnold, Caroline. *Orangutan.* Greenwillow, 1990.

Brockman, Alfred. *Monkeys and Apes: An Animal Fact Book.* Troll, 1986.

Morris, Ann. *Hats, Hats, Hats.* Lothrop, 1989.

Rey, H. A. *Curious George.* Houghton, 1941.

West, Colin. *"Not Me," Said the Monkey.* Harper, 1988.

# Words in a Puzzle

▶ Here are some words from *Caps for Sale.* Read the words. Then find them in the puzzle below. Circle words across or down.

| peddler | ordinary | wares | checked |
|---|---|---|---|
| bunch | straight | disturb | refreshed |
| monkey | finger | angry | stamped |

| B | O | R | D | I | N | A | R | Y | P | K | X | N | D |
|---|---|---|---|---|---|---|---|---|---|---|---|---|---|
| M | P | N | S | V | C | J | E | L | S | S | Y | M | F |
| B | U | N | C | H | D | X | F | F | T | G | J | O | T |
| B | P | E | D | D | L | E | R | R | R | T | K | N | H |
| L | W | Z | B | F | H | G | E | L | A | H | S | K | K |
| Y | M | D | W | A | R | E | S | F | I | N | G | E | R |
| D | P | I | C | D | R | T | H | P | G | K | L | Y | C |
| B | Q | S | S | X | V | K | E | Y | H | D | H | J | M |
| X | S | T | A | M | P | E | D | B | T | B | N | R | V |
| L | T | U | Z | P | S | W | P | D | K | M | F | X | H |
| N | D | R | P | B | C | Y | C | H | E | C | K | E | D |
| Q | W | B | X | C | A | N | G | R | Y | C | Z | T | Y |

▶ Now choose three of the words you circled in the puzzle. Use each word in a sentence. Write the sentences below.

1. _____

2. _____

3. _____

Name _____     Date _____

 # What's for Sale?

▶ Pretend you're a peddler. Draw pictures to show what you would sell and where you would sell it. Draw animals you might meet on your way.

**What I Would Sell**

**Where I Would Sell It**

**Animals I Might Meet on My Way**

▶ What funny thing might happen between you and the animals? Write a story about it or draw a picture in the box below. Share your funny story with your classmates.

# CHARLEY SKEDADDLE

By Patricia Beatty

### SUMMARY

Twelve-year-old Charley is a Bowery Boy—a proud member of one of the toughest New York City street gangs of the 1860s. When his brother is killed in the Civil War, Charley decides to leave New York to join the Union Army. Too young to be a soldier, he takes the job of drummer boy. It is then that he learns the true horror of war. Charley becomes involved in the Battle of the Wilderness, where he sees a good friend killed. Scared and unsure of himself, Charley "skedaddles" from the fighting and heads to the Blue Ridge Mountains, where he meets Granny Bent, a tough mountain woman. Living with Granny, Charley learns the mountain ways, and his self-confidence is restored when he saves Granny's life. As the war comes to an end, Charley must leave the mountains to go west, but he vows to return someday.

## Discussion Sparklers

**1** If you were Charley, would you have run away from the fighting? Tell why or why not.

**2** How was life in the mountains different from Charley's life in New York City? Which life do you think he preferred? Why? Which would you like better? Why?

**3** Do you think Charley ever returned to the mountains? What might he have done in the mountains if he returned?

**4** Imagine that you worked on the Underground Railroad. What might you have done to help slaves escape to freedom in the North?

## FOR YOUR BULLETIN BOARD

Have each student choose one of the following important people from the Civil War era. Ask students to do research on the person, listing facts about his or her life on a large index card. Then invite students to read their cards aloud. Post the cards on a bulletin board labeled "The Civil War Comes to Life."

| | | |
|---|---|---|
| Abraham Lincoln | Robert E. Lee | Ulysses S. Grant |
| Clara Barton | William Sherman | "Stonewall" Jackson |
| Frederick Douglass | Jefferson Davis | George G. Meade |
| Harriet Tubman | John Brown | Harriet Beecher Stowe |

# Fun Fact

Did you know that many Civil War battles have two names? For example, the Battle of Bull Run is also called the Battle of Manassas. The Battle of Antietam is also known as the Battle of Sharpsburg. This is because Confederates named battles after the nearest settlement. Union troops named battles after the nearest landmark, usually a river or a stream.

**Read It Aloud!** Have students work in groups of three. Ask them to read aloud a portion of the story that includes dialogue between two characters. Have one student act as narrator while the others read the character's words, expressing themselves as the characters would.

## Social Studies Connection

Ask students to do research on the causes of the Civil War. Then have small groups of students stage a round-table discussion about the causes of the war. Have half the students in each group take the Northern viewpoint and the other half the Southern viewpoint. You may wish to provide students with blue and gray arm bands to symbolize the blue uniform of the Union troops and the gray of the Confederates. Choose a leader to open each round-table discussion, to monitor it, and to summarize ideas at the close.

**Music Connection** Bring students closer to the Civil War era by playing music and songs from that time. Use a recording such as *Songs of the Civil War* (National Geographic Society, 1976), which provides written lyrics to the songs. Invite students to sing along.

## Physical Education/Art Connection

Stage a "Mountain Field Day," having students participate in games that mountain children might enjoy, such as hopscotch, tug-of-war, jump rope, marbles, pick-up sticks, and checkers. Provide materials such as the following for making homemade toys and games: string, buttons, blocks of wood, yarn, scraps of cloth, paper, beads, clothespins, corks, craft sticks, paper tubes, spools, toothpicks, glue, and rubber bands.

## Other Books to Enjoy

Hunt, Irene. *Across Five Aprils.* Berkley, 1964.

Johnson, Neil. *The Battle of Gettysburg.* Four Winds, 1989.

Kent, Zachary. *The Story of the Surrender at Appomattox Court House.* Childrens, 1987.

Lunn, Janet. *The Root Cellar.* Penguin, 1985.

Reeder, Carolyn. *Shades of Gray.* Macmillan, 1989.

Sabin, Francene. *Harriet Tubman.* Troll, 1985.

# The United States in 1860

This map shows what the United States looked like before the Civil War. There were eighteen free states, fifteen slave states, and territories. Match each state with its abbreviation. Shade or mark the map to indicate free states and slave states. (Notice that Virginia and West Virginia were one state.)

| FREE STATES | | SLAVE STATES | |
|---|---|---|---|
| California | New Hampshire | Alabama | Missouri |
| Connecticut | New Jersey | Arkansas | North Carolina |
| Illinois | New York | Delaware | South Carolina |
| Indiana | Ohio | Florida | Texas |
| Iowa | Oregon | Georgia | Tennessee |
| Maine | Pennsylvania | Kentucky | Virginia |
| Massachusetts | Rhode Island | Louisiana | |
| Michigan | Vermont | Maryland | |
| Minnesota | Wisconsin | Mississippi | |

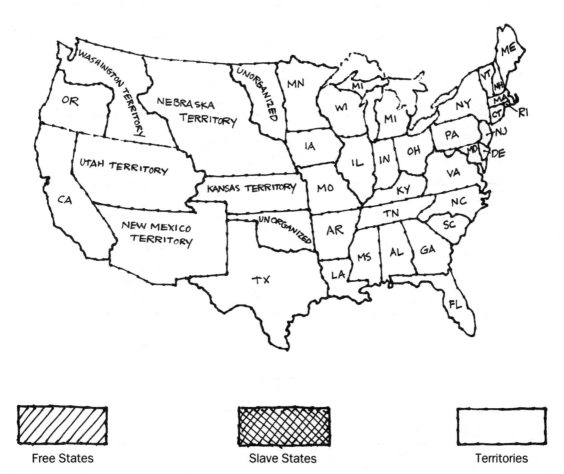

Free States          Slave States          Territories

Name _____                    Date _____

# Granny Bent

▶ Put yourself in Charley's place. Write a paragraph describing how he feels about Granny Bent when he first meets her.

Today I met Granny Bent for the first time. _____

_____

_____

_____

_____

_____

_____

_____

▶ Now write a paragraph describing how Charley feels about Granny Bent on the day he leaves the mountains to head west.

Today I said good-bye to Granny Bent. _____

_____

_____

_____

_____

_____

_____

_____

# CHARLOTTE'S WEB

Written by E. B. White
Illustrated by Garth Williams

## SUMMARY

Wilbur is an endearing pig with some very special friends—a girl named Fern who loves him and cares for him while he is young, a variety of barnyard companions including a self-indulgent rat named Templeton, and a talented spider named Charlotte who becomes his greatest friend of all. When Wilbur learns that he is being fattened up to be killed, Charlotte devises a clever plan to save him. Then before her own death, she leaves behind an egg sac from which hundreds of tiny spiders appear. From then on, Wilbur spends his days at peace in the barnyard, always accompanied by a few of Charlotte's descendents.

## Discussion Sparklers

**1** How were the animal characters in the book like people? In what ways were they like real animals? Which animal character was your favorite? Why?

**2** How did Fern change as the story progressed? Why do you think she changed?

**3** How did Charlotte prove that she was a true friend to Wilbur? How was Wilbur a friend to her?

**4** Was Wilbur really as terrific, radiant, and humble as Charlotte pointed out? Tell why you think he was or wasn't.

## FOR YOUR BULLETIN BOARD

Provide students with advertisements from magazines and newspapers and invite them to find words that they might use to describe Wilbur. Have students paste the words on squares of construction paper. Then post the words on a bulletin board labeled "Some Pig!" You may wish to decorate the board with spider webs that students have drawn with white chalk on dark construction paper.

**Read It Aloud!** *Charlotte's Web* is filled with many humorous events. Have students find a passage that describes something they found particularly funny. Invite students to read their passage aloud.

**Mathematics Connection** Review the schedule that Wilbur created for himself during his first days in the barnyard. Then have students create their own schedule for a typical school day, beginning with the time they get up and ending with the time that they go to bed. Encourage students to list events by the hour and half hour.

**Art Connection** Invite students to make a poster for the county fair that Wilbur attended. Ask them to draw a picture of the fair at the top of the poster. Below the picture, have students write sentences advertising the fair. Encourage them to write at least one sentence about Wilbur, for example: *See the TERRIFIC, RADIANT pig, Wilbur!*

**Music Connection** Draw attention to the lullaby that Charlotte sang to Wilbur at the end of Chapter XIII. Work with students to create a tune for the lullaby. Then ask them to write the lyrics for their own lullaby for Wilbur and set the lyrics to the tune of "Rock-a-Bye Baby."

## Other Books to Enjoy

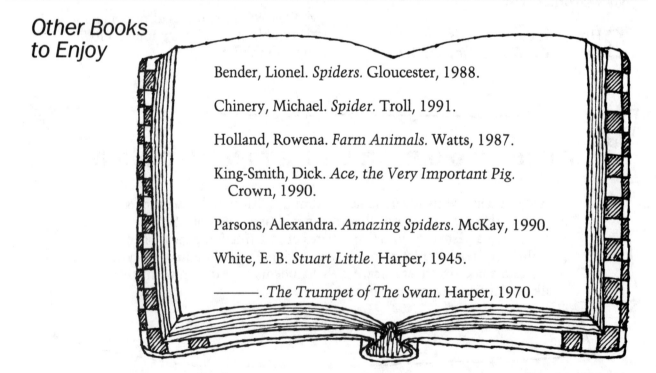

Bender, Lionel. *Spiders.* Gloucester, 1988.

Chinery, Michael. *Spider.* Troll, 1991.

Holland, Rowena. *Farm Animals.* Watts, 1987.

King-Smith, Dick. *Ace, the Very Important Pig.* Crown, 1990.

Parsons, Alexandra. *Amazing Spiders.* McKay, 1990.

White, E. B. *Stuart Little.* Harper, 1945.

————. *The Trumpet of The Swan.* Harper, 1970.

# All About Charlotte

▶ Charlotte wrote words in her webs to describe what a wonderful pig Wilbur was. Now write some words to describe Charlotte. Use a letter in her name to begin each word that you write. Use a dictionary or thesaurus to help you if needed. One example has been done for you.

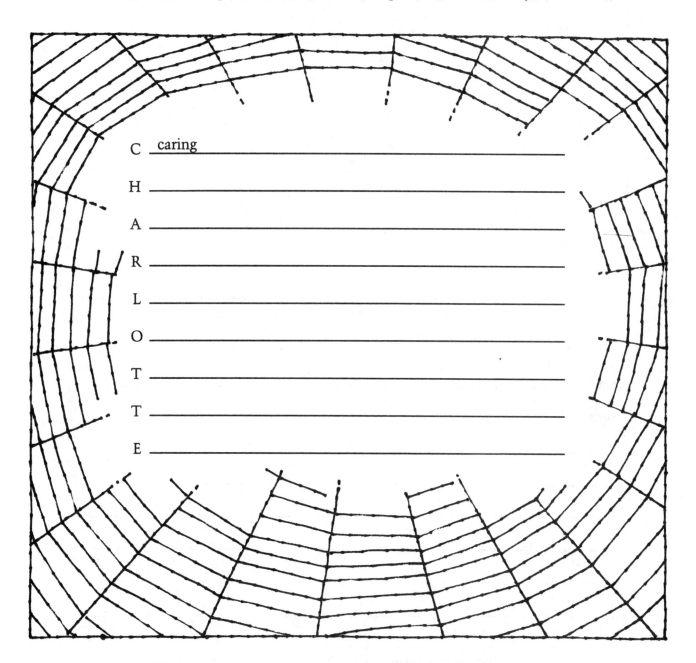

C   caring _____

H   _____

A   _____

R   _____

L   _____

O   _____

T   _____

T   _____

E   _____

▶ Now read your list of words to your classmates. Tell why you chose each word to describe Charlotte.

Name _____     Date _____

# Describe a Season

▶ *Charlotte's Web* includes many beautiful descriptions of the seasons.
What is your favorite season of the year? Draw a picture of that season.
Then write some words to describe that time of the year.

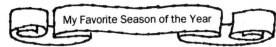
My Favorite Season of the Year

Name of season: _____

Words to describe the season:

_____

_____

_____

_____

_____

_____

▶ Now use the words to write a paragraph that tells about your favorite
season. Write the paragraph on the back of this paper.

# A GATHERING OF DAYS
## A New England Girl's Journal, 1830–32
By Joan W. Blos

### SUMMARY

Given a journal by her father in October of 1830, thirteen-year-old Catherine Hall begins a record of commonplace happenings in her family's rural New Hampshire household as well as of significant events that shape her young life. As her journal progresses, she tells of a fugitive slave that she helps, of her father's remarriage, and of the death of a dear friend. Catherine's descriptions of farm life in New Hampshire reflect the spirit of the New England people, whose lives were filled with hard work, family unity, friendship, and love.

Discussion Sparklers

1 How was life in New England in the 1830s different from life today? Would you like to have lived during those times? Tell why or why not.

2 How would you describe Catherine? Which events helped you to learn about Catherine's character?

3 What were some of the sad times that Catherine experienced? What were some of the happy times that she wrote about? Which events caused her to wonder and worry?

4 Why do you think Catherine gave her journal to her great-grandchild? What information did you learn from her letters to her great-grandchild? What happened to some of the people whom Catherine described in her journal?

# FOR YOUR BULLETIN BOARD

Create a "Gathering of Days" bulletin board to reflect the daily lives of students. Use the bulletin board to display items such as school newsletters, lunchroom menus, classroom notices, announcements of upcoming holidays, schedules of school sports activities, and outstanding work done by students. Encourage students to add to the bulletin board by looking through local newspapers to find articles of interest to the class, the school, and your community. Change the items on the board frequently to keep information current.

# Fun Fact

Some of the highest wind speeds in the world have been recorded in New Hampshire! Mount Washington in the White Mountains of northern New Hampshire is known for its severe weather. In 1934, a record wind of 231 miles (372 km) per hour was recorded at the weather station on the mountain.

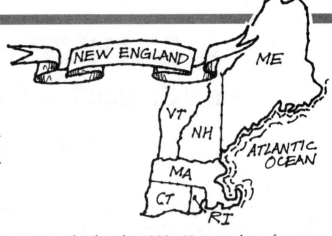

*Read It Aloud!* Help students locate the New England states on a map. Then ask them to choose a journal passage from which they learned something interesting about life in New England in the 1830s. Have students read the journal passages aloud and discuss any unfamiliar words.

## Language Arts Connection

Have students make their own journals by stapling sheets of paper together with a cover made from poster board or construction paper. Provide time for journal writing three or four times a week. Encourage students to include in their journals descriptions of important events as well as personal observations. After about a month, have students read through their journals. Discuss what students learned about themselves through their writing.

## Social Studies Connection

*A Gathering of Days* mentions some of the serious social issues that concerned the people of New England in the 1830s. Have students form two groups. Ask one group to do research on Nat Turner and the slave revolt. Ask the other group to do research on William Lloyd Garrison and his publication, *The Liberator*. Have the groups share with each other the information they learned.

## Mathematics Connection

Review the population figures in Catherine's journal entry of January 24, 1831. Present students with problems to solve based on the figures, for example: *If the population of New Hampshire increased 25,372 in ten years, what was the population in 1821?* or *How many more white females were there in New Hampshire in 1831 than white males?* Then point out that the population of New Hampshire in 1990 was 1,113,915. Have students tell how many more people lived in New Hampshire in 1990 than in 1831.

## Other Books to Enjoy

Bisson, Terry. *Nat Turner*. Chelsea House, 1989.

Blos, Joan W. *Brothers of the Heart: A Story of the Old Northwest, 1837–1838*. Macmillan, 1985.

Harder, Janet D. *Letters from Carrie*. North Country Books, 1980.

Marsh, Carole. *The Hard-to-Believe-But-True! Book of New Hampshire History, Mystery, Trivia, Legend, Lore, Humor & More*. Gallopade, 1990.

———. *New Hampshire Kid's Cookbook: Recipes, How-To, History, Lore & More*. Gallopade, 1990.

# A Gathering of Words

▶ Find three words from *A Gathering of Days* that are unfamiliar to you.
Write the words below and tell where they can be found in the journal.
Use Catherine's journal and a dictionary to help you write the meaning
of each word. Combine your page with your classmates' pages to make a
book titled *A Gathering of Words.*

Word: _____ Journal Entry Date: _____

Meaning of the Word: _____

_____

_____

_____

_____

Word: _____ Journal Entry Date: _____

Meaning of the Word: _____

_____

_____

_____

_____

Word: _____ Journal Entry Date: _____

Meaning of the Word: _____

_____

_____

_____

_____

Name ______________________ Date ____________

# Dear Great-Grandmother

▶ Read Catherine's letter at the back of the book. Catherine wrote it in response to a letter from her great-granddaughter. What do you think Catherine's great-granddaughter's letter said? Write that letter below.

November 25, 1899

Dear Great-Grandmother,

Your loving great-granddaughter,

Catherine

# THE GLORIOUS FLIGHT: ACROSS THE CHANNEL WITH LOUIS BLÉRIOT

Written and Illustrated by Alice and Martin Provensen

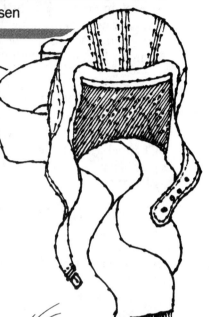

## SUMMARY

One day while Louis Blériot is driving through the city of Cambrai, France, he sees a wonderful airship overhead. The year is 1901, and the airship is an amazing sight. Inspired by the airship, Blériot decides to build a flying machine of his own. He tries many different designs and finally builds an airplane that can really fly. Then Blériot learns that a prize has been offered to the first person who can fly across the English Channel. To prove how good his airplane is, Blériot decides to take the challenge. On July 25, 1909, Blériot climbs into the cockpit of *Blériot XI*. He makes the historic flight across the channel from France to Dover, England, in thirty-seven minutes.

Discussion Sparklers

**1** Do you think Louis Blériot's family approved of him spending so much time building flying machines? Why or why not? What do you think his family thought about him crossing the English Channel?

**2** What words would you use to describe Louis Blériot? Why would you describe him that way?

**3** Have you ever won a prize or an award for being first or the best in something? What did you win? How did winning the prize or award make you feel?

## FOR YOUR BULLETIN BOARD

Ask students to write about one of their own memorable "firsts," such as the first time they rode on a train or a plane, their first time at camp, their first pet, the first time they swam in the ocean, and so on. Encourage students to draw a picture to illustrate their writing. Then post students' work on a bulletin board labeled "Our Glorious Firsts!"

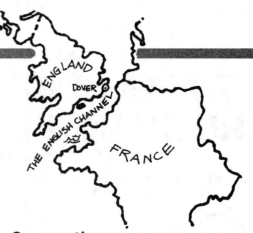

# Fun Fact

The English Channel is called *La Manche* or "the sleeve" in French. The first man to swim across the channel was Matthew Webb in 1875. The first woman was Gertrude Ederle, who made the swim in 14 hours, 31 minutes in 1926.

*Read It Aloud!* Invite groups of students to read aloud the portion of the book that describes Blériot's flight across the English Channel. After the choral reading, discuss how planes have changed over the years since Louis Blériot's flight.

*Social Studies Connection* Display a map or an atlas that shows the English Channel. Have groups of students work together to find England and France and to locate the English Channel. Then ask them to find Dover, England, the place where Louis Blériot landed after his "Glorious Flight."

*Art Connection* Ask students to imagine what they would see if they were flying over their own home in a small plane. Invite them to draw their neighborhood from that point of view.

*Music Connection* Work with students to make up songs about Louis Blériot, creating lyrics to accompany familiar tunes. For example, you might sing a song about Blériot to the tune of "Row, Row, Row Your Boat" (Fly, fly, fly your plane, Over the channel blue . . .) or to the tune of "She'll Be Comin' Round the Mountain" (He'll be flying over the channel when he comes . . .).

*Language Arts Connection* Have students put themselves in Blériot's shoes! Tell them to imagine that they are Louis Blériot and that they have just landed in England after the historic flight over the channel. Ask students to tell what they would say to the crowd of people waiting in Dover.

## Other Books to Enjoy

Balian, Lorna. *Wilbur's Space Machine.* Holiday, 1990.

Livingston, Myra Cohn. *Up in the Air.* Holiday, 1989.

Provensen, Alice and Martin. *Leonardo da Vinci: the Artist, Inventor, Scientist in Three-Dimensional Movable Pictures.* Viking, 1984.

Sabin, Francene. *Amelia Earhart, Adventure in the Sky.* Troll, 1983.

Stein, Conrad R. *The Story of the Spirit of St. Louis.* Childrens, 1984.

Name _____ Date _____

# A Plane of Your Own

▶ Design your own airplane! Make it as unusual as you wish. Draw the plane below and label some of its parts. Give the airplane a name and tell what it can do.

**MY AIRPLANE DESIGN**

The name of my plane is _____ .

What it can do: _____

_____

▶ The book tells you what the great white airship sounded like as it soared over the city of Cambrai. What would your airplane sound like? Write some sound words below.

_____  _____  _____

_____  _____  _____

# Be a Newspaper Reporter!

▶ Write a newspaper story about Blériot's flight across the English Channel. Plan your story by answering the following questions:

• WHO?          _____

• WHAT?         _____

• WHERE?/WHEN?  _____

• WHY?          _____

• HOW?          _____

▶ Now write your story below. Include some words that Blériot might have said.

A Glorious Flight!

by _____ (your name)

DOVER, ENGLAND—

_____

_____

_____

_____

_____

_____

_____

_____

_____

_____

# HAWK, I'M YOUR BROTHER

Written by Byrd Baylor
Illustrated by Peter Parnall

### SUMMARY

Young Rudy Soto wants to fly, but not like just any bird—like a hawk! One day Rudy steals a young hawk from its nest, hoping to learn the special magic of flying. But the young hawk is not meant to live in captivity. Each day it calls to its brothers in the sky and beats its wings against its cage. Finally Rudy realizes that the hawk must be set free. He takes it back to the mountain from which it came and releases it. Free at last, the hawk tests its wings, soars into the air, and calls to Rudy. Rudy calls back with the same hawk sound, and in his mind he is flying too. Now as the days pass, Rudy and the hawk call to each other across the desert, and Rudy knows he is truly brother to the hawk.

**1** Why did Rudy want to fly like a hawk rather than like a wren or a sparrow? Have you watched birds in the air? Did they make you feel as if you wanted to fly? Why?

**2** What does the word *freedom* mean to you? How did giving the hawk its freedom bring Rudy closer to the bird?

**3** What kinds of animals shouldn't be kept as pets? How are those animals different from animals that do make good pets?

**4** Can you think of times when it might be necessary to keep a wild animal in captivity? Give some examples.

## FOR YOUR BULLETIN BOARD

Have students choose a wild animal to "adopt" as a brother or sister. Ask students to draw a picture of that animal and to write the reasons why the animal is special to them. Have them title their papers to reflect the title of the book, for example "Tiger, I'm Your Sister" or "Sea Gull, I'm Your Brother." Display students' work on a bulletin board labeled "Brothers and Sisters of the Wild."

# Fun Fact

Did you know that the peregrine falcon is one of the fastest animals in the world? When a peregrine falcon dives to earth, it can reach speeds as fast as 200 miles (322 km) per hour!

*Read It Aloud!* Have groups of students take turns reading aloud pages from the book. Before students begin, point out the way the lines of the story are arranged. Suggest that students read the lines like poetry—saying each line carefully and with feeling, and pausing whenever they come to a space between the lines.

*Social Studies Connection* Share with students books about the deserts of the United States, pointing out pictures and facts about desert plants and animals. Then have students look through the books and work in pairs to create a desert poster. Ask students to draw a desert scene on their poster and below it write facts about desert plants and animals. Display the posters in the classroom.

*Science Connection* Invite students to become bird watchers. Take a class trip to a nearby park or bird sanctuary to observe the different birds in the area. Have students bring a copy of Activity Sheet 1 with them to record details about the birds they see. As an alternative, you may have students take the Activity Sheet home and observe birds with a member of their family.

*Art Connection* Have students make sand paintings of hawks. Provide students with sterilized sand and poster board or heavy construction paper. The sand and poster board or construction paper should be in contrasting colors. Have students use a paintbrush and glue to paint a picture of a hawk on the paper. Then have them sprinkle sand over the glue and shake off the excess. The pictures may be done in sections so that the glue doesn't dry before the sand is applied. When the sand paintings are complete, display them in the classroom.

*Other Books to Enjoy*

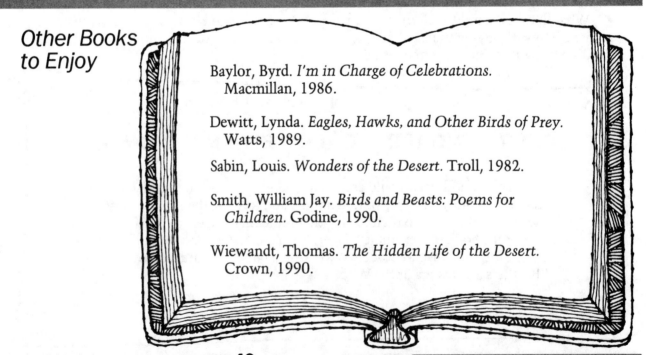

Baylor, Byrd. *I'm in Charge of Celebrations.* Macmillan, 1986.

Dewitt, Lynda. *Eagles, Hawks, and Other Birds of Prey.* Watts, 1989.

Sabin, Louis. *Wonders of the Desert.* Troll, 1982.

Smith, William Jay. *Birds and Beasts: Poems for Children.* Godine, 1990.

Wiewandt, Thomas. *The Hidden Life of the Desert.* Crown, 1990.

Name _____ Date _____

# Be a Bird Watcher

▶ Use the chart below to record information about different kinds of birds you see. Have your teacher or a family member help you name the birds.

### BIRD WATCHER'S CHART

| DATE | WHERE I SAW THE BIRD | NAME OF BIRD (IF KNOWN) AND DESCRIPTION | SOUNDS THE BIRD MADE |
|---|---|---|---|
|  |  |  |  |
|  |  |  |  |
|  |  |  |  |
|  |  |  |  |
|  |  |  |  |

▶ Which bird is your favorite? Draw a picture of that bird below.

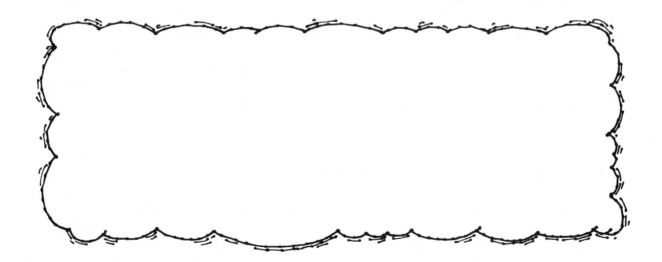

Name _____ Date _____

# Soar with Poetry

▶ Write a poem to a bird. Plan for your poem by writing words that describe birds.

**Words that Describe Birds**

_____ _____ _____

_____ _____ _____

▶ Make your poem rhyme if you wish. Here are some rhyming words you might use. Add some more rhyming words to the list.

wing/sing    fly/sky    soar/more    glide/ride

sail/tail    lift/drift    bird/heard    feather/weather

_____ _____ _____

_____ _____ _____

▶ Write your poem below.

Title: _____

_____

_____

_____

_____

_____

_____

_____

_____

# JUMANJI

Written and Illustrated by Chris Van Allsburg

### SUMMARY

Alone at home and bored, Judy and Peter decide to go to the park across the street to play. There at the foot of a tree they find a long, thin box that contains a jungle game called Jumanji. Taking the game home, they make a horrible discovery—everything that happens in the game also happens in real life. Wild animals invade their home, monsoon rains fall in the living room, and a volcano pours lava through the fireplace! Each roll of the dice brings a new danger, until at last Judy lands in the city of Jumanji and the game ends. Then the dangers fade away, and the children quickly take the game back to the park. When their parents return home with guests, the children say little about what happened. But as they look out the window, they see the sons of a guest running through the park—and one of the boys had a long, thin box under his arm!

Discussion Sparklers

1 How would you have acted if you were Peter and Judy? Would you have done anything differently as you were playing the game? Explain what you might have done.

2 What was in the box that Danny was carrying under his arm at the end of the story? Think about Mrs. Budwing's words,
"They never read instructions either." What might happen when Danny and Walter get home?

3 Have you ever played a game that surprised you or that was much different from what you expected it would be? Tell about that game. How were you surprised?

## FOR YOUR BULLETIN BOARD

Point out the Jumanji box shown on the title page of the book. Encourage students to discuss what they think is pictured on the cover of the box. Then have students draw their own cover for the long, thin box that holds the Jumanji game. Display the pictures on a bulletin board labeled "Jumanji."

**Read It Aloud!** Have students choose the scenes from the book that they thought were the most exciting or the most unusual. Ask partners to read the scenes aloud to each other.

**Art Connection** Discuss with students the illustrations in *Jumanji*, pointing out the way each picture is drawn from an unusual point of view. Next, provide students with charcoal pencils and paper and invite them to draw a black and white picture of a room in their own home. Challenge them to draw the room from an unusual point of view, as Chris Van Allsburg did in his book.

**Social Studies Connection** Suggest that students work in pairs to create their own adventure game set in a different environment, such as the desert, the mountains, a forest, or the ocean. Have students draw a simple game board with a starting point and an ending point. Have them decorate the background of the board with scenes that show the environment they chose. Encourage students to write directions in some of the spaces to make the game similar to Jumanji, for example: *Rattlesnake crosses your path, move back two spaces. Snowstorm in the mountains, lose a turn* or *make friends with a whale, move ahead one space.* Have partners determine simple rules for their game. Then provide them with game pieces and dice and have them play the game together.

**Mathematics Connection** Point out to students that the clocks in Judy and Peter's home have Roman numerals on them. Review with students how to write Roman numerals from 1 to 12. Then challenge them to create simple addition and subtraction problems in Roman numerals. Have students trade problems with partners and solve.

**Language Arts Connection** Invite students to create and recite alliterative phrases that describe animals that might appear in a home during a Jumanji game. Give examples such as: *There's a lion in the laundry room! There's a snake on the snack table! There's a rhino near the refrigerator!* or *There are monkeys on the mantel!*

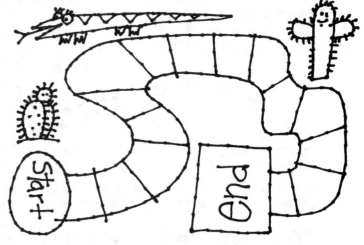

## Other Books to Enjoy

Damon, Laura. *Discovering Earthquakes and Volcanoes.* Troll, 1990.

Petty, Kate. *Lions.* Watts, 1990.

Pope, Joyce. *A Closer Look at Jungles.* Watts, 1984.

Van Allsburg, Chris. *Two Bad Ants.* Houghton, 1988.

Vecchione, Glen. *The World's Best Street and Yard Games.* Sterling, 1989.

# A New Game of Jumanji

▶ What do you think would happen if Danny and Walter played Jumanji in their home? Show some of the moves they might make and tell what would happen after each move. Make their game different from the game that Judy and Peter played—but remember, Jumanji is a *jungle* game.

Danny ⟩ Lands on a space that says: _____

_____

What happens? _____

_____

Walter ⟩ Lands on a space that says: _____

_____

What happens? _____

_____

Danny ⟩ Lands on a space that says: _____

_____

What happens? _____

_____

Walter ⟩ Lands on a space that says: _____

_____

What happens? _____

_____

# Two Different Games

▶ What is your favorite board game? Write the name of that game in the box below. Then tell how it is the same as Jumanji and how it is different.

My favorite board game is _____.

How it is the same as Jumanji: _____

_____

_____

_____

_____

_____

_____

_____

How it is different from Jumanji: _____

_____

_____

_____

_____

_____

_____

_____

_____

# LITTLE HOUSE ON THE PRAIRIE

Written by Laura Ingalls Wilder
Illustrated by Garth Williams

### SUMMARY

In *Little House on the Prairie*, Laura Ingalls Wilder tells the story of her family's move from the Big Woods of Wisconsin to the prairies of Kansas. Pa Ingalls has decided that the Big Woods is too crowded, so he and the rest of the family—Ma, Mary, Laura, baby Carrie, and Jack the bulldog—head west in a covered wagon to "Indian country." The journey is long and sometimes dangerous, but the family finally finds a good spot on the prairie to build a home. There, life is filled with new experiences, including encounters with the Indians, who are both frightening and fascinating to young Laura. Eventually the government decides to move all settlers out of Indian Territory, and the Ingallses must leave their little prairie home. They pack up their belongings, say good-bye to the other settlers, and head out in the wagon once more.

## Discussion Sparklers

**1** How do you think Laura felt when she had to leave her home and her relatives in Wisconsin to move west to a part of the country that was just being settled? How would you feel?

**2** Why do you think the Ingalls family was never harmed by the Indians who came to their home or who rode past the house on their horses? How did Pa feel about the Osage chief named Soldat du Chêne?

**3** What do you think might have happened to Laura and her family after they left their home on the prairie? How would you feel if you had to leave a home that you worked so hard to build?

## FOR YOUR BULLETIN BOARD

Display a map of the United States on a bulletin board labeled "From Wisconsin to Kansas." Have students work in groups to find a route that the Ingalls family might have taken from Wisconsin, through Minnesota, Iowa, and Missouri, to their prairie home near the Verdigris River and Independence, Kansas. Then make a trip to the library to have students do research on the Osage Indians. Have students write their findings on index cards and post them on the bulletin board next to the map.

# Fun Fact

The covered wagons that the pioneers used were also called "prairie schooners." They were given that name because the white canvas tops on the wagons made them look like sailing ships crossing the open prairie.

*Read It Aloud!* Ask students to find passages in the book that they found interesting or exciting. Invite students to read the passages aloud. Encourage students to comment on the passages they read, telling how they would feel if they were a member of the Ingalls family at the time.

*Social Studies Connection* Invite students to interview adult family members or older friends to find out about interesting trips that they took when they were young. Have students write a description of one of the trips, telling where the person went and how he or she traveled. Encourage students to illustrate their writing. Then have them share their work by reading it aloud. You may also wish to invite some of the family members or friends to come to the class to tell about their trips.

*Art Connection* Ask students to draw a covered wagon similar to the one in which the Ingalls family traveled. Have them label parts of the wagon, such as the canvas top, wagon bows, wagon box, running gear, wagon seat, and wagon tongue. Display the drawings in the classroom and discuss with students how the Ingallses used parts of their wagon to help them build their prairie home.

*Music Connection* Pa loved to play his fiddle and sing! If possible, play a recording that includes a variety of songs from the pioneer days, such as *Westward Ho!* (National Geographic, 1977), or have students join in with you to sing some familiar pioneer songs. Songs that you might sing include "Oh, Susanna," "Hush, Little Baby," "Old Dan Tucker," "Skip to My Lou," "Sweet Betsy from Pike," and "Clementine."

## Other Books to Enjoy

Collins, James L. *Exploring the American West.* Watts, 1989.

George, Jean Craighead. *One Day in the Prairie.* Harper, 1986.

Sabin, Francene. *Pioneers.* Troll, 1985.

Sabin, Laurence. *Oregon Trail.* Troll, 1985.

Wilder, Laura Ingalls. *Little House in the Big Woods.* Harper, 1953.

———. *On the Banks of Plum Creek,* Harper, 1953.

# Pack Your Wagon

▶ Make a list of the things that you would take with you if you were crossing the country in a covered wagon in the 1870s. Remember, covered wagons were not very big, so choose your items carefully!

Food and Cooking Utensils

_____
_____
_____
_____
_____
_____
_____

Clothing and Bedding

_____
_____
_____
_____
_____
_____
_____

Tools

_____
_____
_____
_____
_____
_____

Other Important Things

_____
_____
_____
_____
_____
_____

# Dear Diary

▶ Choose two important days in Laura's life. Write a diary entry for each day as Laura might have written it.

Dear Diary,

Dear Diary,

# THE PAPER CRANE

Written and Illustrated by Molly Bang

### SUMMARY

One evening a stranger comes into the empty restaurant of a poor man. Although the stranger has no money, the restaurant owner cooks a wonderful meal for him and serves him like a king. To repay the kindness, the stranger makes a magical paper crane that comes to life and dances whenever the owner claps his hands. Soon people from all over come to eat at the restaurant and see the bird perform. Then one evening the stranger returns. Without saying a word, he takes out a flute and begins to play, and the crane dances as never before. Then the stranger climbs on the back of the crane and they fly away. Although they are never seen again, people continue to gather at the restaurant to eat and hear stories of the magical bird.

**Discussion Sparklers**

1 Look at the pictures at the beginning of the book that look like photographs in an album. What do you learn about the restaurant by looking at those pictures?

2 What parts of this story could happen in real life? What parts could never happen?

What does this story tell you about friendship and helping others?

3 Who was the boy in the story? Why do you think the boy was playing a flute in the last picture of the book?

## FOR YOUR BULLETIN BOARD

Point out the way the author used three-dimensional figures to illustrate her book. Then have students cut out from poster board figures of people. Have them complete the figures by drawing faces on them and gluing on yarn for hair and colorful scraps of wrapping paper or cloth for clothes. When the figures are complete, display them on a bulletin board labeled "New Guests for the Paper Crane Restaurant."

**Act It Out!** Invite small groups of students to act out the story, playing the parts of the owner, the boy, the stranger, the crane, and the guests in the restaurant. You may wish to have students improvise the performance, or act out the story as you or a student read the narration aloud. Provide students with props to use during their performance.

**Social Studies Connection** Point out the picture of the highway construction plan that shows the restaurant and the new highway that was built close by. Then ask students to draw a map of the neighborhood in which they live. Encourage them to label their home and the streets or highways that are nearby.

**Music Connection** Play a recording of flute music and invite students to dance as the paper crane danced in the book. Then ask volunteers to do their paper crane dance alone while the other students imitate it.

**Mathematics Connection** Assemble students in groups and ask each group to create a simple lunch, breakfast, or dinner menu for a restaurant. Have students work together to suggest items for the menu and to decide on a price for each item in dollars and cents. Then have students write the menu on chart paper. Post the menus on a classroom wall and provide students with play money. Call out items from the menu and have students show the coins or bills they would need to buy each item.

**Art Connection** Explain to students that origami is the Japanese art of paper folding. Encourage students to experiment with folding paper to create objects of their own design. Then provide them with books that show simple origami figures to make. Have students create an origami figure, such as a flower or a bird.

## Other Books to Enjoy

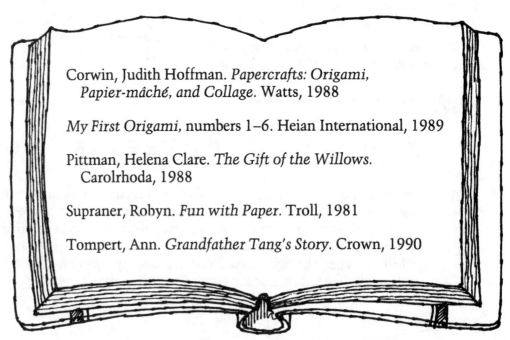

Corwin, Judith Hoffman. *Papercrafts: Origami, Papier-mâché, and Collage.* Watts, 1988

*My First Origami,* numbers 1–6. Heian International, 1989

Pittman, Helena Clare. *The Gift of the Willows.* Carolrhoda, 1988

Supraner, Robyn. *Fun with Paper.* Troll, 1981

Tompert, Ann. *Grandfather Tang's Story.* Crown, 1990

# My Favorite Restaurants

▶ Draw pictures of two of your favorite restaurants. Tell what you like to eat at each one.

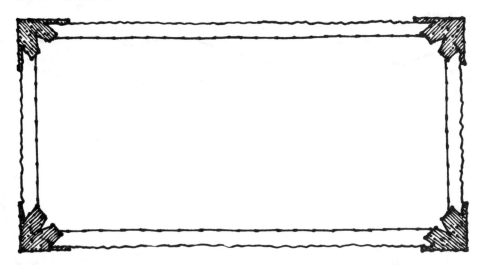

The name of the restaurant is _____.

This is what I like to eat there:

_____

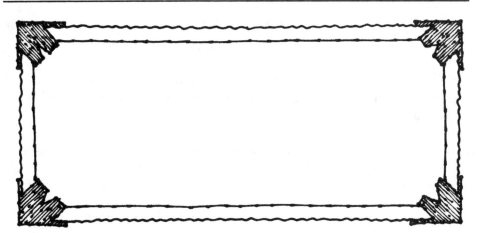

The name of the restaurant is _____.

This is what I like to eat there:

_____

_____

# Where Did They Go?

▶ Where do you think the stranger and the paper crane went after they flew out of the restaurant? Draw a picture to show where they might have gone.

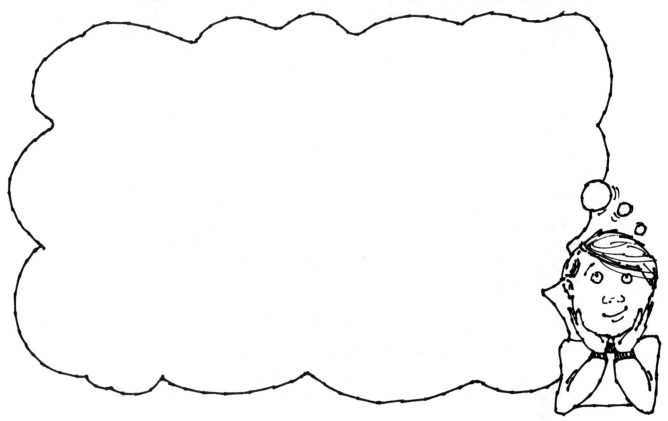

▶ What do you think the stranger and the paper crane did when they got to the place in your picture? Write your ideas below or tell them to your classmates.

_____

_____

_____

_____

_____

_____

_____

# THE PATCHWORK QUILT

Written by Valerie Flournoy
Illustrated by Jerry Pinkney

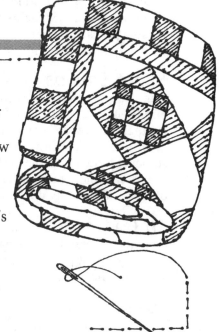

## SUMMARY

Why is a patchwork quilt special? Tanya's grandmother knows. A patchwork quilt never forgets. It can tell your life story. When Grandma decides to make a new patchwork quilt, Tanya is delighted. Tanya's mother helps sew the quilt as Grandma cuts the patches, using squares of cloth from different family members. Then one day Grandma falls ill, and the family takes over the quilt making. Mama, Tanya, and even Tanya's brothers help, but it is Tanya who does most of the work. She even adds a piece of Grandma's old quilt to the new one. Eventually, Grandma grows stronger, and she takes up her quilting again. She finishes the quilt with a special last touch—delicate stitching in the corner that says, "For Tanya from your Mama and Grandma."

Discussion Sparklers

**1** How did Mama feel about the quilt when Grandma first began to make it? How did Mama's feelings change? How did the quilt bring Mama closer to Grandma?

**2** How do you think the family felt when Grandma became ill? What might have made Grandma grow stronger again?

**3** Why do you think Tanya's grandmother gave her the quilt? How do you think Tanya felt when she discovered that the quilt would be hers? How would you feel?

## FOR YOUR BULLETIN BOARD

Remind students that when Tanya's Grandma made her quilt, she took scraps of cloth from clothing that was important to the members of her family. Invite students to draw a picture of their own family. Tell them to show each family member dressed in an article of clothing that is special to him or her in some way. Display the pictures on a bulletin board labeled "Special Family Memories."

**Read It Aloud!** Have students work in small groups to read aloud passages from *The Patchwork Quilt*. Students may take turns reading pages or paragraphs from the passage, or they may read the entire passage aloud together.

**Social Studies Connection** Christmas was a very special holiday for Tanya and her family. Ask students what holidays are special for them. Have them draw a picture of their favorite holiday. Below the picture, have students write the name of the holiday, the month in which it occurs, and a brief description of what their family does on that day.

**Art Connection** Invite students to work together cooperatively to make a class "Friendship Quilt." Provide them with large squares of heavy white paper and have each student draw a self-portrait on a square. Ask students to sign their name on a corner of the square. To make the quilt, have students piece their picture squares together with squares of construction paper. The squares may be taped together to form the quilt, or the quilt may be assembled by taping the squares to a classroom wall.

**Mathematics Connection** Give students graph paper with large squares. Have them color the squares with different colors or

different designs to make the paper look like a quilt. Then ask students to tell how they can figure out the total number of squares on the paper. Lead them to recognize that they could count every square, they could add the number of squares in each row, or they could multiply the number of squares across by the number of squares down. Have students choose a method for determining the total number of squares and demonstrate it to a partner.

**Language Arts Connection** Ask students to imagine that they are one of Grandma's grandchildren who live far away. Then give them construction paper and have them design a get-well card for Grandma. On the front of the card, have students draw a cheerful picture. On the inside of the card, have them write a get-well message for Grandma.

**Other Books to Enjoy**

Coerr, Eleanor. *The Josefina Story Quilt*. Harper, 1986.

Johnston, Tony. *The Quilt Story*. Putnam, 1985.

Livingston, Myra Cohn. *Poems for Grandmothers*. Holiday, 1990.

Mayne, William. *The Patchwork Cat*. Knopf, 1981.

Polacco, Patricia. *The Keeping Quilt*. Simon & Schuster, 1988.

# Through the Seasons

▶ *The Patchwork Quilt* tells about Tanya's family during different seasons of the year. What are the seasons like where you live? Draw pictures to show the seasons. Write what you like to do during each time of the year.

**Spring**

In the spring I _____

_____

_____.

**Summer**

In the summer I _____

_____

_____.

**Fall**

In the fall I _____

_____

_____.

**Winter**

In the winter I _____

_____

_____.

Name _____     Date _____

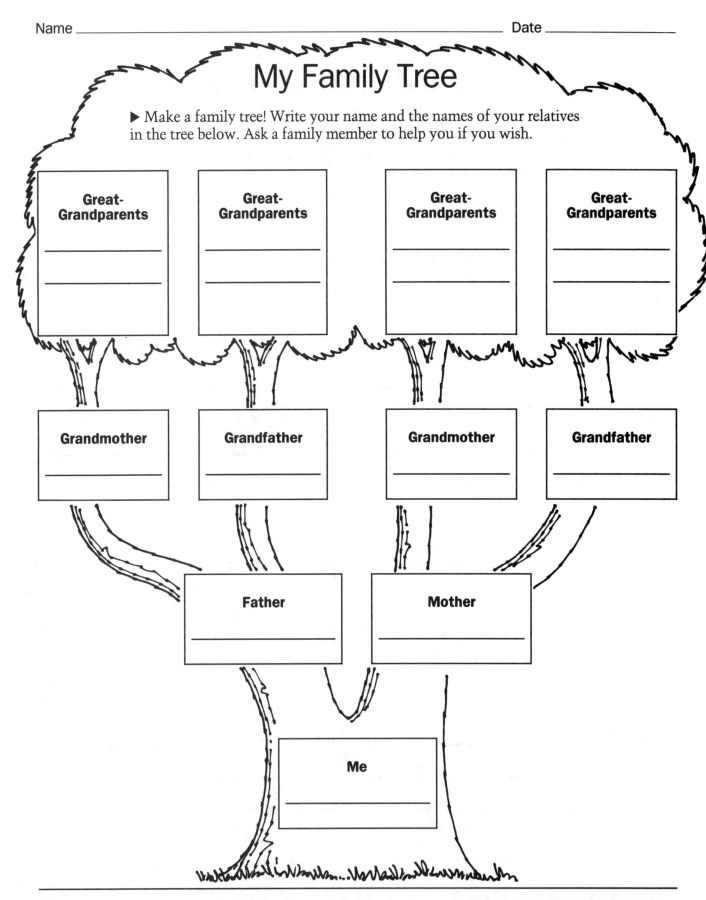

# My Family Tree

▶ Make a family tree! Write your name and the names of your relatives in the tree below. Ask a family member to help you if you wish.

**Great-Grandparents**
_____
_____

**Great-Grandparents**
_____
_____

**Great-Grandparents**
_____
_____

**Great-Grandparents**
_____
_____

**Grandmother**
_____

**Grandfather**
_____

**Grandmother**
_____

**Grandfather**
_____

**Father**
_____

**Mother**
_____

**Me**
_____

# SARAH, PLAIN AND TALL

## By Patricia MacLachlan

### SUMMARY

The 1986 Newbery Award winner *Sarah, Plain and Tall* tells the story of Anna and Caleb, whose mother has died, and of Sarah, who comes from Maine to stay with them and their father. When Papa places an ad for a wife in the newspapers, Sarah answers. Then she comes to visit them in their home on the prairie to see what life is like there. During her visit, Sarah wins the hearts of Papa and the children, but she misses her home in Maine and longs for the sea. Will Sarah stay? The children grow fearful when Sarah leaves in the wagon. But Sarah returns, bringing with her drawing pencils in the colors of the sea and the reassurance that even though she will always miss her old home, she would miss them more if she left them.

## Discussion Sparklers

**1** What is the setting for this story? Describe the time and the place. What information from the book gave you clues about the setting?

**2** When Sarah came from Maine, she brought Caleb a shell and Anna a sea stone. Why do you think she decided to bring those things to the children? What would you bring from your home to give to someone you had never met before?

**3** Imagine that Sarah, Papa, and the children made a visit to Maine after the wedding. What might happen during that visit? What would the children see there?

## FOR YOUR BULLETIN BOARD

When Sarah wrote to Papa, she described herself as "plain and tall." What two words would students use to describe themselves? Invite students to draw a self-portrait. Below their pictures, have students describe themselves in two words. Encourage students to use complimentary words, for example: *Michael, Quick and Athletic; Luisa, Cheerful and Smart; Jason, Funny and Friendly.* Display the pictures on a bulletin board labeled "Our Class, Special and Spectacular!"

# Fun Fact

Suppose you wanted to travel to the easternmost part of the United States. Where would you go? To Maine! West Quoddy Head, a small peninsula in Maine, is farther east than any other place in the United States.

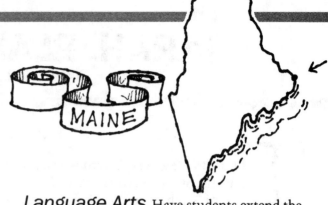

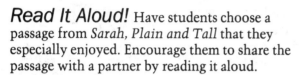

**Read It Aloud!** Have students choose a passage from *Sarah, Plain and Tall* that they especially enjoyed. Encourage them to share the passage with a partner by reading it aloud.

**Science Connection** Display a variety of seashells for students to examine, or ask students to bring seashells from home. Explain that the shells belong to animals called mollusks, and point out univalves (one shell, such as snails) and bivalves (two halves, such as clamshells). Have students sort the shells according to appearance and encourage them to describe how the shells look and feel. Then invite students to put to their ear a shell such as a conch to "hear" the sea. Explain that what students are hearing is not really the sea, but the movement of air through the shell.

**Language Arts** Have students extend the story by writing a brief episode in which they describe the wedding of Sarah and Papa. Suggest that students tell about the people and animals that might be at the wedding, where the wedding might be held, and what the characters might say to each other. Encourage students to share their writing by reading it aloud.

**Social Studies Connection** Display a map of the United States and have students locate Maine. Have them find the capital city of Augusta, as well as other large cities such as Bangor, Lewiston, and Portland. Then invite students to speculate on the area from which Sarah might have come. Have them give reasons for their responses.

## Other Books to Enjoy

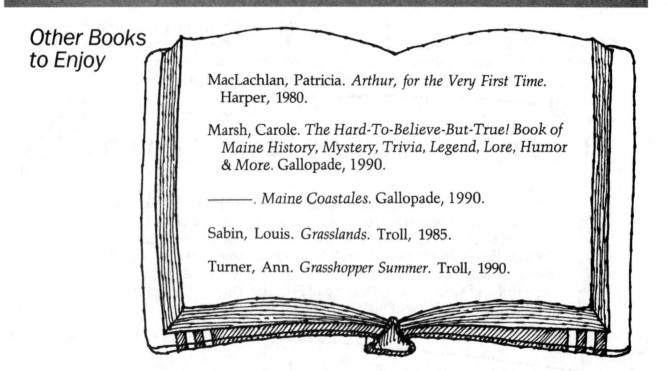

MacLachlan, Patricia. *Arthur, for the Very First Time.* Harper, 1980.

Marsh, Carole. *The Hard-To-Believe-But-True! Book of Maine History, Mystery, Trivia, Legend, Lore, Humor & More.* Gallopade, 1990.

———. *Maine Coastales.* Gallopade, 1990.

Sabin, Louis. *Grasslands.* Troll, 1985.

Turner, Ann. *Grasshopper Summer.* Troll, 1990.

# Two Different Worlds

▶ Sarah found that living on the prairie was very different from living near the sea. Compare the two areas on the chart below. Use the descriptions in the book to help you list some of the plants and animals from each place and to tell about the land.

| Near the Sea | On the Prairie |
|---|---|
| Animals: _____ | Animals: _____ |
| _____ | _____ |
| _____ | _____ |
| _____ | _____ |
| Plants: _____ | Plants: _____ |
| _____ | _____ |
| _____ | _____ |
| _____ | _____ |
| The Land: _____ | The Land: _____ |
| _____ | _____ |
| _____ | _____ |
| _____ | _____ |

▶ Would you rather live near the sea or on the prairie? Tell why.

_____

_____

_____

_____

Name _____ Date _____

# My Own Favorite Place

▶ At the end of the book, Sarah brought the family pencils that were the colors of the sea—blue, gray, and green. What three colors would you use to draw a picture of your favorite place? Write the names of those colors on the pencils below.

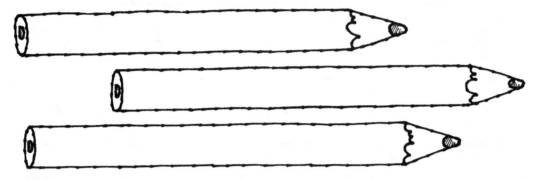

▶ Now draw a picture of your favorite place using those colors.

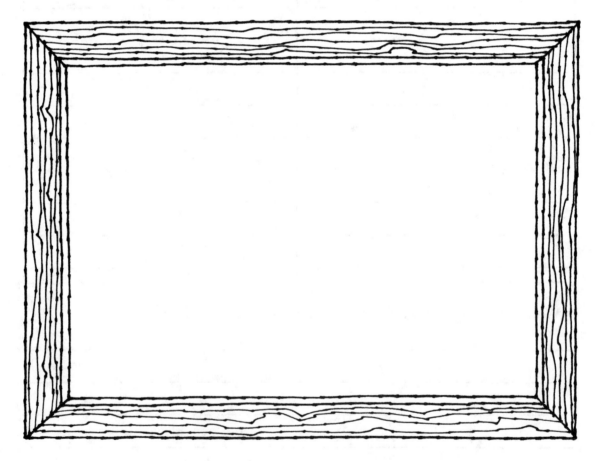

# A STORY, A STORY

Retold and Illustrated by Gail E. Haley

## SUMMARY

*A Story, A Story* is an African tale that explains how "Spider Stories" came to be. Ananse, the Spider man, wants the stories that Nyame, the Sky God, keeps in a golden box near his royal stool. The "price" that Nyame asks for the stories is that Ananse bring him Osebo the leopard, Mmboro the hornets, and Mmoatia the fairy-whom-men-never-see. Although Ananse is old and weak, he is very clever. He captures the leopard, the hornets, and the fairy by using his tricks. Then he spins a web around them and pulls them up into the sky. Nyame praises Ananse for what he has done and proclaims that his stories now belong to Ananse and will be called "Spider Stories" from that day on. Ananse takes the stories back to earth, where they scatter to the corners of the world.

## Discussion Sparklers

**1** What did you learn about African stories from this book? How can you let a story come and then let it go?

**2** Why do you think Ananse wanted the stories that belonged to the Sky God? What did he do with those stories?

**3** Does this story about Ananse remind you of any other stories that you've heard or read? What stories does it remind you of? Explain why.

## FOR YOUR BULLETIN BOARD

Have students make word webs to describe Ananse. Ask them to write Ananse's name in the center of a piece of paper. Around the name, have them write words to tell what Ananse was like. You may wish to model the activity by beginning a word web such as the one shown. Post the students' word webs on a bulletin board labeled "Ananse, the Spider Man."

# Fun Fact

Not all leopards are tan with dark spots. There are also black leopards, which are sometimes called black panthers. These black leopards also have spots, but the spots are hard to see in the leopard's dark fur.

*Read It Aloud!* Invite groups of students to present *A Story, A Story* as Readers' Theater. Have one member of each group act as storyteller, or narrator. Other members of the group may read aloud the parts of Ananse, Nyame, the leopard, the hornets, Mmoatia the fairy, and the nobles of the court. Encourage students to read their parts with expression, saying the words as the characters themselves might have said them.

*Mathematics Connection* Invite students to play a game of "Put the Spots on the Leopard." Have students work in small groups to draw the outline of a large leopard on chart paper or butcher paper. Then provide each group with twenty to fifty "spots"—flat, round objects such as counters or pennies. Have students take turns taking a handful of "spots" and tossing them onto the leopard one at a time, trying to place as many spots on the leopard as possible. After each student's turn, ask group members to estimate how many spots landed on the leopard and how many landed outside. Have students count the spots to verify their estimates.

*Language Arts Connection* Cover a large box with gold paper and fill it with books for students to read. Invite students to go to the "golden box" to choose books. Have them share the stories they read by retelling them. You might label a chair the "Royal Stool" and have students sit on it while retelling the stories.

*Art Connection* Have groups of students work together to create a diorama of the jungle world that is shown in the book. Provide students in each group with a large box and have them decorate the inside of the box with jungle scenes that they have drawn on paper. Additional plants for the jungle may be cut out from green construction paper and glued on the jungle floor. Then provide students with modeling clay or dough and have them create small figures of Ananse, the leopard, and the fairy to display in their diorama. A paper or clay version of the hornet nest may be hung inside the box with string or yarn.

## Other Books to Enjoy

Aardema, Verna. *Rabbit Makes a Monkey of Lion*. Dial, 1989.

Appiah, Peggy. *Tales of an Ashanti Father*. Beacon, 1981.

Haley, Gail E. *Sea Tale*. Dutton, 1990.

Kimmel, Eric A. *Anansi and the Moss-Covered Rock*. Holiday, 1988.

McDermott, Gerald. *Anansi, the Spider: A Tale from the Ashanti*. Holt, 1972.

Name _____ Date _____

# African Animals

▶ Ananse captured a leopard and some hornets and spun a web around them. What other animals might Ananse catch in Africa? Draw three African animals in the web below.

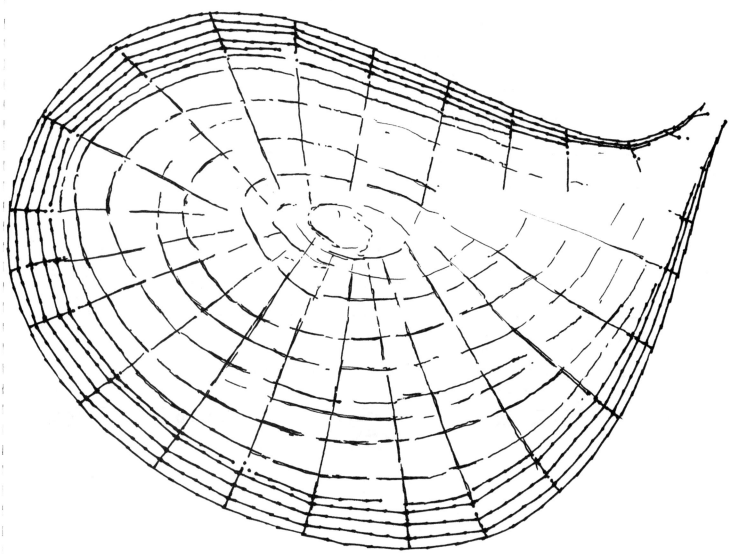

▶ What kind of sound does each animal make? Write the sounds below.

Name of the Animal                          Sound It Makes

_____          _____

_____          _____

_____          _____

# My Story, My Story

▶ Make up a new story about Ananse. In your story, tell about something else that Ananse wants from the Sky God. Plan for your story by answering these questions:

What does Ananse want from the Sky God?

_____

_____

What must he bring the Sky God in return?

_____

_____

How will he get the things he must bring the Sky God?

_____

_____

_____

▶ Draw pictures to show how your story begins and ends. Then tell your story to your classmates.

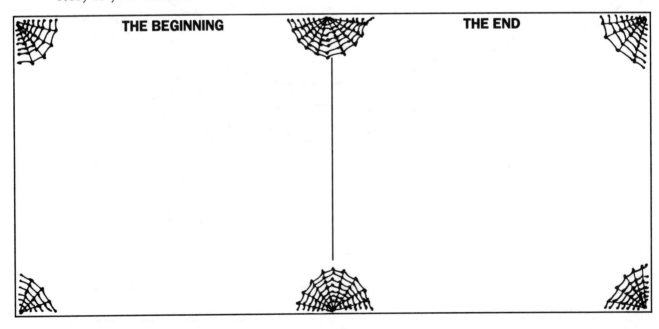

**THE BEGINNING**          **THE END**

# A VISIT TO WILLIAM BLAKE'S INN
## Poems for Innocent & Experienced Travelers
Written by Nancy Willard
Illustrated by Alice and Martin Provensen

## SUMMARY

Take a trip to an imaginary inn run by the English poet William Blake. There you'll make a number of unusual acquaintances—dragons who bake the bread, angels who wash and shake featherbeds, the King of Cats, the man in the marmalade hat, and others! Introduced to Blake at an early age, the author of the Newbery Award–winning *A Visit to William Blake's Inn* has used her knowledge and love of Blake to create a wonderful collection of poems that spark the imagination while celebrating the poet and his works.

## Discussion Sparklers

1 The works of William Blake inspired Nancy Willard to write this book of poems. Have you ever been inspired by the work of an author, a poet, or an artist? What did that work inspire you to do?

2 Which poem in the book is your favorite? Why do you like that poem? Which characters are your favorites?

3 How do the pictures in the book add to your enjoyment of the poems? Would you like to visit William Blake's Inn? Tell why or why not.

4 Think about Blake's advice to travelers that appears at the end of the book. What do you think he meant by those words?

## FOR YOUR BULLETIN BOARD

Point out the fanciful vehicles pictured in *A Visit to William Blake's Inn.* Tell students to look carefully at the pictures and name the different ways that each vehicle might move about. Then ask students to create their own fanciful vehicle to take them to William Blake's Inn. Encourage them to draw vehicles that can move in more than one way. Display the drawings on a bulletin board labeled "On Our Way to William Blake's Inn!"

# Fun Fact

William Blake was an English poet and painter who lived from 1757 to 1827. He spent most of his life in London, where he worked as a book illustrator and engraver. The poem by Blake that Nancy Willard heard from her baby sitter is called "The Tyger." It is one of Blake's best-known poems.

**Read It Aloud!** Use *A Visit to William Blake's Inn* to offer students opportunities for a variety of read-aloud experiences. Individual students may read aloud poems to the class; students might join in together to recite a poem; and partners may read aloud poems together.

**Language Arts Connection** Ask students to write a letter to either the poet who created the book, Nancy Willard, or to the illustrators of the book, Alice and Martin Provensen. In their letters, have students name their favorite poem or illustration and tell the poet or the illustrators why they liked the book. Encourage students to read their letters aloud.

**Music Connection** Invite students to recite with you the poem titled "The Marmalade Man Makes a Dance to Mend Us." Then have students work in pairs or small groups to set the poem to music. Have students create their own tune to go with the words of the poem, and encourage students to sing their version of the poem to their classmates.

## Other Books to Enjoy

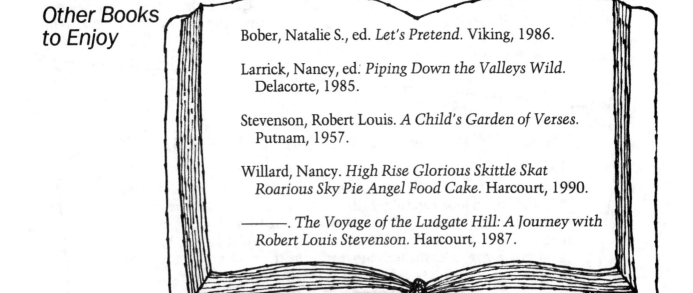

Bober, Natalie S., ed. *Let's Pretend*. Viking, 1986.

Larrick, Nancy, ed. *Piping Down the Valleys Wild*. Delacorte, 1985.

Stevenson, Robert Louis. *A Child's Garden of Verses*. Putnam, 1957.

Willard, Nancy. *High Rise Glorious Skittle Skat Roarious Sky Pie Angel Food Cake*. Harcourt, 1990.

———. *The Voyage of the Ludgate Hill: A Journey with Robert Louis Stevenson*. Harcourt, 1987.

# An Inn of My Own

▶ Pretend that you own a magical inn. What people, animals, and plants would be guests at your inn? Draw those guests below. Give your inn a name.

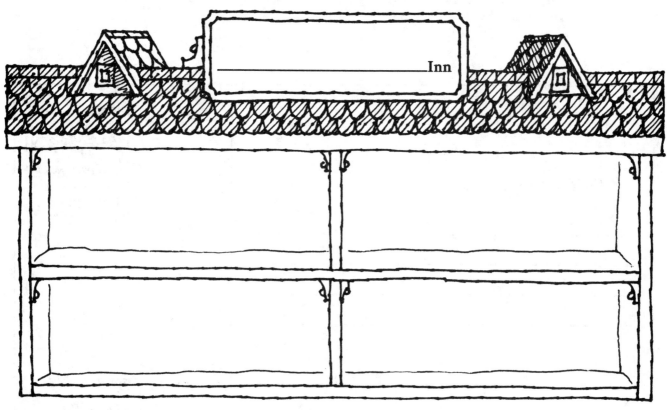

_____ Inn

▶ Make a list of your guests' names in the Guest Register below.

**Guest Register**

_____

_____

_____

_____

_____

_____

_____

_____

Name _____  Date _____

# The King of Cats and His Wife

▶ Read the poem that tells what the King of Cats wrote on his postcard to his wife. Notice that the first two lines in each verse rhyme and that the second two lines rhyme. Then pretend you are the King of Cats' wife. Answer your husband by writing a postcard in two verses. Try to make your lines rhyme as he did.

*Dearest Husband,*

_____
_____
_____
_____
_____
_____

*Your wife,*
*The Queen of Cats*

TWO PENCE

*POSTCARD*

*To: The King of Cats*
*William Blake's Inn*

# THE WEDNESDAY SURPRISE

Written by Eve Bunting
Illustrated by Donald Carrick

## SUMMARY

On Wednesday nights when Anna's mother stays late at the office and her brother goes to basketball practice, Anna's grandma comes to watch her. The nights are special for the two. They talk and read together, and one night they plan a special birthday surprise for Anna's father. On Dad's birthday, he comes home tired after driving his truck all night. While Dad sleeps, the family prepares for the celebration, and Grandma arrives with a big bag of books. Finally it's time for the party! After Dad blows out his birthday candles and opens his gifts, Anna and Grandma reveal their special surprise. Anna opens Grandma's bag, gives Grandma a book, and Grandma begins to read. Everyone is astonished—except Anna, because every Wednesday night while the others were away, Anna had been teaching her grandmother to read!

## Discussion Sparklers

**1** Did *The Wednesday Surprise* surprise you? What did you think Anna and Grandma's surprise would be?

**2** Anna and Grandma both knew that reading is very important. How can knowing how to read help a person every day?

**3** Why do you think Grandma said it's smarter to learn to read when you're young? Why was it still important for her to learn to read even though she wasn't young?

## FOR YOUR BULLETIN BOARD

Have students draw the outline of a book on construction paper and cut it out. Invite them to write the name of their favorite book on the cutout or draw a picture to show an important scene in the book. Ask students to write their name at the bottom of the cutout. Then post the cutouts on a bulletin board labeled "Our Favorite Books." Encourage students to go to the bulletin board to discover new books to read that their classmates have already enjoyed.

# Fun Fact

The Library of Congress in Washington, D.C., has over 20 million books. There are more than 530 miles (855 km) of bookshelves in the library, which also contains millions of records, engravings, maps and atlases, photographs, motion pictures, and other reference materials.

**Read It Aloud!** Invite students to take turns reading aloud pages from the book. As an alternative, students may read passages from the book with you, joining in whenever they can.

## Mathematics Connection

Have students name the days of the week in order from Sunday to Saturday, as well as the months of the year from January to December. Then provide them with a blank calendar grid such as the one shown. Spell out the days of the week at the top of the calendar and designate the first day of the current month with the numeral 1. Then write the name of the current month on the chalkboard and have students copy the name at the top of their calendar. Have them write the remaining dates of the month in order.

| Sunday | Monday | Tuesday | Wednesday | Thursday | Friday | Saturday |
|--------|--------|---------|-----------|----------|--------|----------|
|        |        |         |           |          |        |          |
|        |        |         |           |          |        |          |
|        |        |         |           |          |        |          |
|        |        |         |           |          |        |          |
|        |        |         |           |          |        |          |

## Social Studies Connection

Point out the bus-stop sign at the beginning of the book and discuss the importance of signs with students. Ask them questions such as "How do signs help us?" and "What kind of information can we learn from reading signs?" Then have students name some road signs that Anna's father might see as he drives his truck, for example: stop signs, speed limit signs, highway exit signs, advertising signs, rest stop signs, crosswalk signs. Invite students to draw pictures of signs that they have recently seen. Have them display their signs and talk about the kind of information that the signs give.

## Language Arts Connection

Point out to students that the family's pet cat is shown in many of the pictures in the book. Invite students to pretend that the cat can talk. Ask them to retell the story as the cat might tell it. Have students work in small groups to tell the cat's story orally, or have them work individually to write the story on paper. (You may wish to have students complete Activity Sheet 1 on page 73 before they complete this activity.)

## Other Books to Enjoy

Aliki. *How a Book Is Made.* Harper, 1986.

Curtis, Gavin. *Grandma's Baseball.* Crown, 1990.

Gibbons, Gail. *Check It Out: The Book About Libraries.* Harcourt, 1985.

Levinson, Nancy Smiler. *Clara and the Bookwagon.* Harper, 1988.

Silverman, Erica. *On Grandma's Roof.* Macmillan, 1990.

# Beginning, Middle, and End

▶ What happens in *The Wednesday Surprise?* Draw a picture to show a scene from the beginning, the middle, and the end of the story. Write a sentence to tell what happens.

### THE BEGINNING

What happens: _____

### THE MIDDLE

What happens: _____

### THE END

What happens: _____

Name _____ Date _____

# Plan a Surprise Party!

▶ Plan a pretend surprise party for someone in your family. Write the
name of the person. Then draw or write to finish the page.

A Surprise Party for _____

▶ Draw or write the names of two presents for the person.

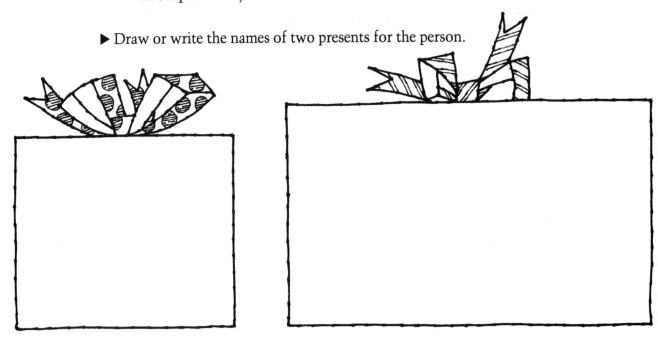

▶ Draw or write the names of foods that you would serve at the party.

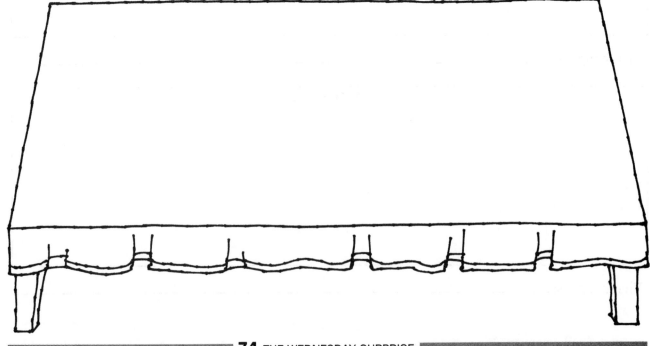

# WHEN I WAS YOUNG IN THE MOUNTAINS

Written by Cynthia Rylant
Illustrated by Diane Goode

## SUMMARY

In *When I Was Young in the Mountains*, the narrator remembers all the things that made growing up in the mountains a very special experience. Life was simple, but filled with love. Grandfather came home from the coal mines covered with black dust and kissed her on the top of the head. Grandmother cooked wholesome food, and baths were taken in round tin tubs filled with water from the well. Crawford's store supplied fresh butter and other goods, and people went to church in the schoolhouse on Sundays. Evenings were special times when the family sat on the porch swing while stars sparkled in the sky and a bobwhite whistled in the woods. When the narrator was young in the mountains, she never longed to travel, for living in the mountains was always enough.

## Discussion Sparklers

**1** Why was the girl's home in the mountains special to her? Do you think you would like to grow up in the mountains? Tell why or why not.

**2** How do you think the girl felt about her grandmother and grandfather? What clues do the pictures and the story give you about her feelings?

**3** The girl says that when she was young in the mountains, she never wanted to go anywhere else. Why do you think she felt that way? Have you ever wanted to travel to other parts of the world? Where would you like to go and why?

## FOR YOUR BULLETIN BOARD

Point out to students that the narrator of *When I Was Young in the Mountains* has many happy memories of life in the mountains with her family. Then invite students to draw a picture of a happy time that they've had with family members or close friends. Ask students to write sentences below the picture to tell what happened, or have students display their picture in class and talk about the happy time. Post the pictures on a bulletin board labeled "Happy Memories."

**Read It Aloud!** Have students take turns reading aloud pages from the book. You might also read the book aloud with students, having them supply the phrase "When I was young in the mountains" whenever it appears.

**Social Studies Connection** Explain to students that the author of the book spent her childhood in the Appalachian Mountains of West Virginia. Then display a map of the United States and point out the Appalachian Mountains. Explain that the Appalachian Mountains include different mountain ranges, such as the Catskill Mountains in New York, the Smoky Mountains in Tennessee and North Carolina, and the Blue Ridge Mountains, which run from Georgia to Pennsylvania. Point out those mountain ranges on the map. Then have students find where the Appalachian Mountains are located in West Virginia.

**Mathematics Connection** Set up a country store in the classroom. Have students bring in empty boxes and containers from home, such as egg cartons, cereal boxes, coffee tins, clean jelly jars, and soap boxes. Display the empty boxes and containers on a shelf in the classroom and have students help you label the items with price tags that show dollars and cents. Then provide students with play money and have them "shop" at the store. Have students take turns being the store owner who takes the money and gives change.

**Science Connection** Draw attention to the pictures of the black snake in the book, and encourage students to talk about what they know about snakes. Then have students work in small groups to find out more. Provide them with an encyclopedia or books about snakes and have them find names of poisonous and nonpoisonous snakes, as well as other interesting facts about snakes. Have each group make a poster entitled "What We Know About Snakes" on which they draw pictures of snakes and list facts about them. Display the posters on a classroom wall.

**Cooking Connection** Point out the picture of the family having a meal of corn bread, pinto beans, and fried okra. Explain to students that okra is a vegetable that is shaped like a pod, and ask them if they have ever tried it. If possible, display pictures of okra and dried pinto beans for the students to examine. Then invite students to make their own corn bread. Supply them with the ingredients and utensils and have groups mix batches of corn bread in class. Bake the corn bread for students in an oven in the school cafeteria and enjoy it as a special snack.

**Other Books to Enjoy**

Hendershot, Judith. *In Coal Country*. Knopf, 1987.

Hirschi, Ron. *Who Lives in . . . the Mountains?* Putnam, 1989.

Lauber, Patricia. *Snakes are Hunters*. Harper, 1989.

Levinson, Riki. *I Go with My Family to Grandma's*. Dutton, 1986.

Rylant, Cynthia. *Henry and Mudge and the Bedtime Thumps*. Bradbury, 1991.

————. *The Relatives Came*. Bradbury, 1985.

Name _____  Date _____

# The Same or Different

▶ Tell how your life is the same as or different from the girl's life in the book. Write sentences, or draw pictures and tell about them.

[ _____ ]  ♡  [ _____ ]

The girl lived with her grandparents.
I live with

[ _____ ]  ♡  [ _____ ]

The girl shopped in a country store.
I shop at

[ _____ ]  ♡  [ _____ ]

The girl took baths in a round tin tub.
I take baths in

[ _____ ]  ♡  [ _____ ]

The girl spent evenings sitting on the porch swing.
I spend evenings

# Home Sweet Home

▶ Write the name of your city or town below. Then draw a picture of your home. Write why you like living where you do, or tell your classmates why you like it.

_____
(name of your city or town)

## What My Home Looks Like

Why I like living where I do:

_____
_____
_____
_____
_____
_____

# WHERE THE BUFFALOES BEGIN

Written by Olaf Baker
Illustrated by Stephen Gammell

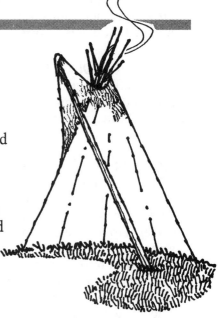

### SUMMARY

First published in 1915, *Where the Buffaloes Begin* tells the story of young Little Wolf and his desire to find the place "where the buffaloes begin." According to tribal legend, the buffaloes have their beginnings beneath a great lake to the south, and it is to that lake that Little Wolf journeys. There, at night, Little Wolf sees an amazing sight. Hundreds of buffaloes rise out of the lake in front of him. Little Wolf cries out to the animals in wonder, and they stampede onto the prairie, sweeping him north toward the camp of his people. When he nears the camp, Little Wolf sees a band of enemy warriors who are about to attack. Little Wolf cries out to the buffalo again, and they head for the warriors and trample them. From that day on, Little Wolf's name is added to the legend of the lake because he led the buffaloes to save his people.

1 What do you think drove Little Wolf to seek the great lake to the south? Have you ever had an idea that would not go away until you investigated it? How did you feel and what did you do?

2 What words would you use to describe Little Wolf? How do you think the people of his village felt about him before he went to the great lake? How do you think they felt about him after he led the buffaloes?

3 This story was first published in 1915. Why do you think the story is still popular with readers today?

## FOR YOUR BULLETIN BOARD

Ask students to imagine how Nawa, the wise man, would tell the legend of the lake after Little Wolf led the buffaloes to save his people. Have students write the legend as they think it would be told and illustrate their writing with a picture of Little Wolf and the buffaloes. Display students' work on a bulletin board labeled "The Legend of the Great Lake."

# Fun Fact

The American buffalo is not a true buffalo. This brownish-black animal with its shaggy head and humped shoulders is correctly known as a bison.

### Read It Aloud! *Where the Buffaloes Begin* is filled with many descriptive passages. Ask students to choose a passage that brings a vivid picture to their minds and have them read it aloud.

### Social Studies Connection In the mid-1800s, 20 to 30 million bison, or American buffaloes, roamed the prairies. By the end of the 1800s, the bison were almost extinct. Invite students to do research on the bison. Have them write a brief report on how and why the great numbers of bison changed during the 1800s. In their report, have them also tell about the status of bison in the United States today. Encourage students to read their reports aloud.

### Art Connection Point out the picture of the pair of moccasins that appears near the beginning of the book and explain to students that the Native Americans of the plains often decorated their moccasins with beautiful beadwork. Then have students trace outlines of their shoes on chart paper. Have them design a pair of moccasins on the outlines, drawing an original pattern for beadwork.

### Language Arts Connection Explain to students that a chant is a type of poem in which lines are repeated over and over again. The lines of a chant have a strong beat that makes the words seem almost musical. Give the following example of a chant. Then have students write and recite their own chant about Little Wolf.

He went to the great lake in the south.
  Little Wolf saved his people.
He saw the buffaloes rise from the lake.
  Little Wolf saved his people.
He rode with the buffaloes to the north.
  Little Wolf saved his people.
He led the buffaloes against his foes.
  Little Wolf saved his people.

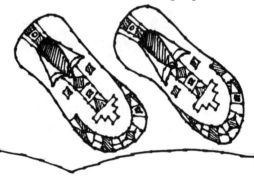

## Other Books to Enjoy

Cohlene, Terri. *Quillworker, A Cheyenne Legend.* Watermill, 1990.

Fleischer, Jane. *Pontiac, Chief of the Ottawas.* Troll, 1979.

Freedman, Russell. *Buffalo Hunt.* Holiday, 1988.

Goble, Paul. *Beyond the Ridge.* Bradbury, 1989.

Gregory, Kristiana. *The Legend of Jimmy Spoon.* Harcourt, 1990.

Ziter, Cary B. *The Moon of Falling Leaves: The Great Buffalo Hunt.* Watts, 1988.

Name _____ Date _____

# In Little Wolf's Words

▶ Imagine that you are Little Wolf. Tell the story of your adventure with the buffaloes. Use words such as *I, me, my,* and *mine* to make your writing a first-person narrative.

**The Day I Saved My People**
by Little Wolf

_____
_____
_____
_____
_____
_____
_____
_____
_____
_____
_____
_____
_____
_____
_____
_____
_____
_____
_____

# Use Your Senses

▶ What did Little Wolf see, feel, hear, and smell when he first saw the buffaloes rising out of the lake?

Little Wolf saw _____

_____ .

Little Wolf felt _____

_____ .

Little Wolf heard _____

_____ .

Little Wolf smelled _____

_____ .

▶ Now name a memorable experience that you once had. Tell what you saw, felt, heard, and smelled at that time.

My Experience: _____

I saw _____

_____ .

I felt _____

_____ .

I heard _____

_____ .

I smelled _____

_____ .

# THE WHIPPING BOY

Written by Sid Fleischman
Illustrated by Peter Sis

## SUMMARY

The Newbery Award–winning *The Whipping Boy* tells the story of an orphan boy named Jemmy who is taken into a royal household to act as whipping boy for a spoiled young prince. Whenever the prince (known as Prince Brat throughout the kingdom) needs to be punished, Jemmy must take the whipping for him. Then one day the prince decides to run away from home. He commands Jemmy to go with him, and they begin an adventure in which they are captured and pursued by two unsavory characters known as Hold-Your-Nose Billy and Cutwater. Eventually the boys escape the villains and return to the castle safely. The adventure makes the prince a more considerate boy, and in the end he and Jemmy become true friends and companions.

## Discussion Sparklers

1 Why do you think the prince was so spoiled? How did he change after his adventure with Jemmy? Would you like to have the prince or Jemmy as your friend? Tell why.

2 Which part of the book was the most exciting to you? Which part was the funniest? Did the author's note at the back of the book surprise you? Why or why not?

3 What do you think happened to Hold-Your-Nose Billy and Cutwater after they stowed away on the convict ship? Do you think they might return to the kingdom someday? What do you think they would do if they did return?

## FOR YOUR BULLETIN BOARD

Ask students to think about what they would do if they were a prince or a princess for a day. Then provide them with yellow construction paper and invite each student to draw and cut out a royal crown. On their crown, have students write what they would do as prince or princess and sign their name. Display the crowns on a bulletin board labeled "Princes and Princesses for a Day."

**Act It Out!** Invite groups of students to choose a scene from the book to act out for their classmates. Encourage them to study the scene in the book closely before their performance and then improvise the scene using words that the characters would say.

**Music Connection** Suggest that students pretend that they are "ballad sellers." Have them work in small groups to create a ballad about Jemmy and the prince. Encourage them to use as a model the song that the ballad seller sang about Hold-Your-Nose Billy in Chapter 18. Invite groups to sing their ballads for their classmates.

**Language Arts Connection** On the chalkboard begin a Venn diagram such as the one below. Have students help you fill in the diagram by naming ways Jemmy and the prince are alike and different. Then have students create their own Venn diagram in which they compare and contrast Hold-Your-Nose Billy and Cutwater. Encourage students to display their diagrams and explain them.

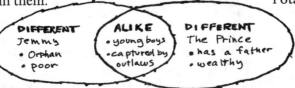

**Art Connection** Provide students with butcher paper and have them work in groups to make murals of the waterside fairgrounds. Before students begin the mural, encourage them to study the illustration in Chapter 18 and skim the chapter to find names of participants at the fair, such as the juggler, stilt walker, acrobats, harp player, seller of live fowl, hot-potato man, cow lady, ballad seller, news seller, and Betsy and her bear, Petunia. Display the completed murals on a classroom wall under the banner "The Waterside Fairgrounds."

**Physical Education Connection** Have groups of students play a game of "Hot Potato" in honor of Captain Nips, the hot-potato man. Give each group a soft ball to toss as the "hot potato." Then set a timer for several minutes and have students stand in a circle and toss the ball to one another. When the timer goes off, the student who is holding the ball is stuck with the "hot potato" and must walk around the circle calling out "Potatoes, Potatoes, Hot Potatoes for Sale!"

## Other Books to Enjoy

Aliki. *The King's Day: Louis XIV of France.* Crowell, 1989.

Fleischman, Sid. *The Case of Princess Tomorrow.* Random House, 1981.

Grimm, Brothers. *Twelve Dancing Princesses.* Troll, 1979.

Landon, Lucinda. *Meg Mackintosh and the Mystery at the Medieval Castle: A Solve-It-Yourself Mystery.* Little, Brown, 1989.

Wilde, Oscar. *The Happy Prince.* Simon & Schuster, 1989.

# Adventure Time

▶ Create a new adventure for Jemmy and the prince. Use the Adventure Planner below to help you.

## ADVENTURE PLANNER

Where will the adventure take place?

_____

What new characters will Jemmy and the prince meet?

_____

_____

_____

What will happen in the adventure? Write the events in order.

Use the back of the page if necessary.

1. _____

_____

2. _____

_____

3. _____

_____

4. _____

_____

5. _____

_____

▶ Now use your Adventure Planner to help you tell your adventure story to your classmates.

# What's New

▶ When Jemmy and the prince went to the fairgrounds, they met a news seller who was calling out the news of the day. What news do you know that would interest your classmates? Write a news story below and draw a picture to illustrate it. Remember to answer the questions *Who? What? Where? When? Why?* and *How?* when you write the story.

## THE CLASSROOM DAILY

"All the News That's News Today"

(Draw your picture above.)

HEADLINE: _____

BY: _____ (your name)

_____

_____

_____

_____

_____

_____

▶ Now read your news story aloud to your classmates and show them the picture you drew.

# WHY CAN'T YOU UNSCRAMBLE AN EGG?

Written by Vicki Cobb
Illustrated by Ted Enik

## S U M M A R Y

Which weighs more, a pound of feathers or a pound of gold? Why does an ice cube float? How much does air weigh? Why can't you unscramble an egg? Answers to these and "other not such dumb questions about matter" are explained in this fascinating book. Filled with easy-to-perform experiments, the book gives simple explanations for phenomena around us. From experiments with water and air to learning how a chemical reaction can happen in your own mouth, *Why Can't You Unscramble an Egg?* makes learning about scientific principles fun.

**Discussion Sparklers**

1 What interesting things about matter did you learn from this book? What things surprised you? What things did you already know?

2 *Why Can't You Unscramble an Egg?* lists a number of chemical reactions that go on around us every day. What other chemical reactions can you name?

3 The book tells us that if there weren't any chemical reactions, there wouldn't be life on earth. How do chemical reactions help keep us alive?

# F O R   Y O U R   B U L L E T I N   B O A R D

Write the name of each of the following elements on a large index card. Write the symbol for each element on another card.

| gold Au | silver Ag | oxygen O | nitrogen N |
| hydrogen H | carbon C | iron Fe | neon Ne |

Display all the cards on a bulletin board labeled "Eight Elements." Post the names of the elements at the top of the board and the symbols at the bottom. Then challenge students to match each element with its symbol. As students give the correct answers, move the cards to the middle of the board so that the name of each element is next to its symbol.

*Read It Aloud!* Have students find passages from the book that tell about experiments that they can perform themselves. Ask students to read those passages aloud.

*Science Connection* Assemble materials needed to perform some or all of the experiments in the book. Then provide students with copies of page 89 and invite them to work in groups to perform the experiments. If groups are performing different experiments, have them share the results of those experiments with one another. If they are performing the same experiment, have them compare results.

*Cooking Connection* *Why Can't You Unscramble an Egg?* describes a baking cake as a "hotbed of reactions." Demonstrate this for students by assembling the ingredients needed to bake a cake from scratch. Have students describe the appearance of each ingredient. Then have students help you mix the cake and pour it into a pan or cupcake tins. Talk about how the ingredients change when they are mixed. Next, use the oven in the school cafeteria to bake the cake. Invite students to taste the cake and tell how the ingredients changed once more. Ask questions such as "What did heat do to the cake ingredients?", "Why did the cake rise?" and "Why can't we change the ingredients back to their original form?"

*Language Arts Connection* Point out the picture of the girl reading the story "Rumpelstiltskin" in the section titled "How Can You Make Gold?" Have students discuss their knowledge of the story. Then obtain a copy of "Rumpelstiltskin" and read it aloud with students. Discuss with them why gold could never really be spun from straw.

*Other Books to Enjoy*

Adler, David. *Amazing Magnets.* Troll, 1983.

Cobb, Vicki. *Bet You Can! Science Possibilities to Fool You.* Greenwillow, 1990.

————. *Why Doesn't the Earth Fall Up? And Other Not Such Dumb Questions About Motion.* Lodestar Books, 1989.

Gardner, Robert. *Science Around the House.* Messner, 1989.

Penrose, Gordon. *Sensational Science Activities with Dr. Zed.* Simon & Schuster, 1990.

Supraner, Robyn. *Science Secrets.* Troll, 1981.

Wong, Ovid K. *Is Science Magic?* Childrens, 1989.

Name _____ Date _____

# Try It Yourself!

▶ Try some of the experiments in the book yourself. Use this form for each experiment you do.

Name of Experiment: _____

Materials Used: _____

_____

What I Think Will Happen:

_____

_____

Procedure for Experiment:

1. _____

   _____

2. _____

   _____

3. _____

   _____

4. _____

   _____

5. _____

   _____

What Actually Happened:

_____

_____

_____

# What's Your Answer?

▶ Look at the questions that are listed in the table of contents of *Why Can't You Unscramble an Egg?* Choose three questions that you can answer now that you have read the book. List the questions below and write an answer in your own words.

Question: _____

Answer: _____

_____

_____

_____

Question: _____

Answer: _____

_____

_____

_____

Question: _____

Answer: _____

_____

_____

_____

# WILL YOU SIGN HERE, JOHN HANCOCK?

Written by Jean Fritz
Illustrated by Trina Schart Hyman

☆ ☆ ☆ ☆ ☆ ☆ ☆ **SUMMARY** ☆ ☆ ☆ ☆

Who was the first person to sign the Declaration of Independence? John Hancock, of course! But there are many other interesting facts and stories about John Hancock's life, as this lively book points out. As a boy, John seemed to have everything. He was raised by a rich uncle and inherited a fortune at the age of twenty-seven. But John always wanted more. With the help of Samuel Adams, John entered public office. From then on, he was to make his mark on American history. *Will You Sign Here, John Hancock?* is filled with fascinating information about this intriguing man and his many accomplishments.

## Discussion Sparklers

**1** The book points out that John Hancock wanted to be liked by *everybody*. Would you have liked John Hancock as a friend? Tell why or why not.

**2** In your opinion, what were the most important things that John Hancock did during his lifetime? What were some of the foolish things?

**3** Do you think John Hancock died a happy man? Give reasons for your answer.

## FOR YOUR BULLETIN BOARD

As *Will You Sign Here, John Hancock?* points out, John loved to dress in rich, flashy clothes. Point out the picture of John in his fancy waistcoat that appears next to the second page of the text. Then invite students to design their own waistcoat for John. Have them draw the waistcoat on paper and color it. Encourage students to make the waistcoat as "flashy" as they wish. Display students' work on a bulletin board labeled "Fancy Waistcoats for John Hancock."

# Fun Fact

Where is the Declaration of Independence today? It is preserved at the National Archives Building in Washington, D.C., along with two other very important documents, the United States Constitution and the Bill of Rights.

### Social Studies Connection

Encourage students to work in small groups to do research on the Revolutionary War. Have them take notes to record information about the causes of the war, where the first shots were fired, the important people of the era, and how the war ended. Ask students to share their findings with other groups by reading their notes aloud.

### Mathematics Connection

Present students with story problems based on the life of John Hancock, for example: *When John Hancock was elected governor in 1780, he won 9,475 votes out of 10,383. How many voters did not vote for John Hancock?* (908 voters) *John Hancock ordered 6 dozen pewter dishes after he became governor. How many dishes did he order in all?* (72 dishes) *If John Hancock was born in January 1737 and died in October 1793, how old was he when he died?* (56 years old)

### Language Arts Connection

Display a facsimile of the Declaration of Independence. Have students locate John Hancock's name on the document as well as other well-known men of the time, such as Thomas Jefferson *(Th. Jefferson)*, Benjamin Franklin *(Benj. Franklin)*, and Samuel Adams *(Saml. Adams)*. Next, read aloud the beginning of the text of the document. Ask students what they think the signers of the Declaration of Independence meant by the words: *We hold these truths to be self-evident, that all men are created equal, that they are endowed by their Creator with certain unalienable Rights, that among these are Life, Liberty and the pursuit of Happiness.*

## Other Books to Enjoy

Fradin, Dennis. *John Hancock: First Signer of the Declaration of Independence.* Enslow, 1989.

Frith, Michael. *Autographs! I Collect Them!* McKay, 1990.

Fritz, Jean. *Can't You Make Them Behave, King George?* Putnam, 1982.

————. *Shh! We're Writing the Constitution.* Putnam, 1987.

————. *What's the Big Idea, Ben Franklin?* Putnam, 1976.

————. *Why Don't You Get a Horse, Sam Adams?* Putnam, 1974.

Morris, Richard B. *The American Revolution.* Lerner, 1985.

Sabin, Francene. *Freedom Documents.* Troll, 1985.

Santrey, Laurence. *Thomas Jefferson.* Troll, 1985.

# John Hancock's Life

▶ John Hancock was born in January 1737 and died in October 1793.
What important events happened to John Hancock during his life?
Record some of those events in the time line below.

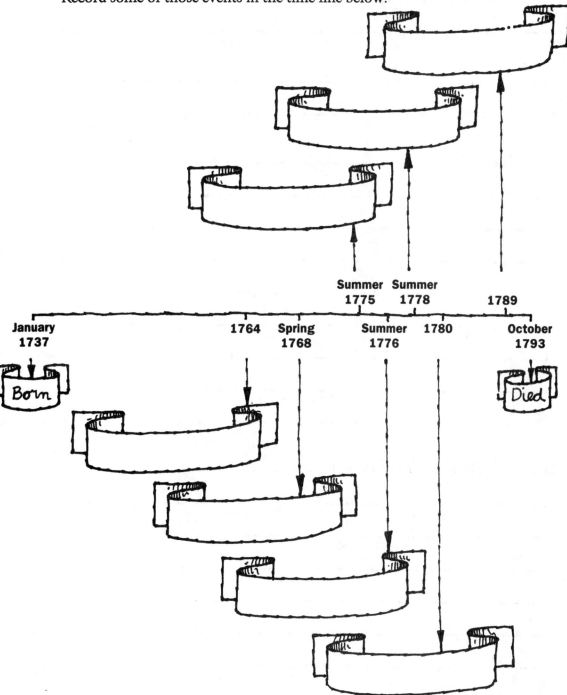

Summer 1775  Summer 1778  1789

January 1737    1764    Spring 1768    Summer 1776    1780    October 1793

Born

Died

# My Autobiography

▶ A biography is the story of a person's life as written by another person. An autobiography is a person's own story of his or her life. What would you write in your autobiography? Complete the page with some autobiographical facts.

I was born on _____

in the city/town of _____ .

My earliest memories are: _____

_____

_____

_____

_____

_____

_____

_____

_____

Today I live in _____ .

Some interesting facts about me today are: _____

_____

_____

_____

_____

_____

_____

_____

Name _____  Date _____

# My Book Report

Title of Book _____

Author _____

▶ Complete the sentences. Draw pictures in the picture frames.

My favorite character was _____.

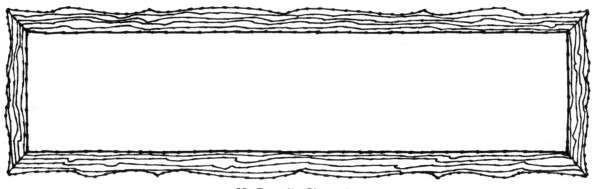

**My Favorite Character**

My favorite part of the book was _____

_____.

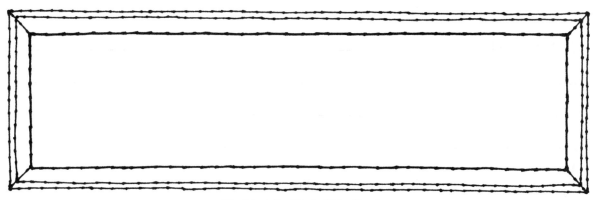

**My Favorite Part of the Book**

▶ Circle words to describe the book.
I think the book was _____.

| | | |
|---|---|---|
| very good | good | not very good |
| funny | sad | boring |
| interesting | scary | silly |
| too long | too short | just right |

Name _____ Date _____

# Book Report

TITLE: _____

AUTHOR: _____

ILLUSTRATOR: _____

Main Character(s): _____

_____

Setting (Time/Place): _____

_____

Summary of What Happens: _____

_____

_____

_____

_____

My Favorite Part of the Book: _____

_____

_____

_____

Why the Author Wrote the Book: (circle one)

To Entertain          To Inform          To Entertain and Inform

## OPINION SCALE (circle a number)

| 1 | 2 | 3 | 4 | 5 | 6 | 7 | 8 | 9 | 10 |
|---|---|---|---|---|---|---|---|---|----|

1 = Book is not very good.          10 = Book is great!